access to history

in depth

VOTES
for WOMEN
1860–1928

Second Edition

Paula Bartley

Dedication: for Kate Karalius

Orders: please contact Bookpoint Ltd, 130 Milton Park, Abingdon, Oxon OX14 4SB. Telephone: (44) 01235 827720. Fax: (44) 01235 400454. Lines are open from 9.00 - 6.00, Monday to Saturday, with a 24 hour message answering service. You can also order through our website www.hodderheadline.co.uk.

British Library Cataloguing in Publication Data
A catalogue record for this title is available from the British Library

ISBN 0 340 857 919

First Published 2003
Impression number   10 9 8 7 6 5 4 3 2 1
Year   2009 2008 2007 2006 2005 2004 2003

Cover photo courtesy of the British Library.

Produced by Gray Publishing, Tunbridge Wells.
Printed in Great Britain for Hodder & Stoughton Educational, a division of Hodder Headline Plc, 338 Euston Road, London NW1 3BH by Bath Press Ltd.

Contents

Preface   v
Acknowledgements   vii

Chaper 1   Introduction: Change and Continuity in the
                Position of Women, 1860–1918   1
                1 Education   2
                2 Work   3
                3 Marriage   4
                4 Sexual Morality   6
                5 Politics   6
                Study Guide   9

Chapter 2   Votes for Women: The Debate   10
                1 The Case for Votes for Women   11
                2 The Case Against Votes for Women   21
                3 Conclusion   27
                Study Guide   30

Chapter 3   Suffragists and Suffragettes   32
                1 The Origins of Women's Suffrage   33
                2 The NUWSS and its Offshoots: 1897–1914   36
                3 The WSPU and its Offshoots: 1903–14   40
                4 Conclusion   48
                Study Guide   52

Chapter 4   The Suffrage Campaigns   55
                1 Introduction   56
                2 Legal Methods   57
                3 Illegal Methods   67
                4 Conclusion   74
                Study Guide   76

Chapter 5   Men and Votes for Women   79
                1 The Political Parties   80
                2 The Liberal Government 1906–14   85
                3 The Alternative Establishment   91
                4 Male Organisations   94
                5 Conclusion   98
                Study Guide   102

Chapter 6   Women, Suffrage and the First World War   105
                1 The Suffrage Movement and the War   106
                2 Women's War Work and the Vote   112
                3 War, Suffrage and the Government   114
                4 Conclusion   117
                Study Guide   119

Chapter 7   Conclusion: Life after Suffrage   122
              1 The Effects of the Vote   122
              2 Effects on Parliament   123
              Study Guide   134

Further Reading   136
Index   141

Preface

To the general reader

Although the *Access to History* series has been designed with the needs of students studying the subject at higher examination levels very much in mind, it also has a great deal to offer the general reader. The main body of the text (i.e. ignoring the 'Study Guides' at the ends of chapters) forms a readable and yet stimulating survey of a coherent topic as studied by historians. However, each author's aim has not merely been to provide a clear explanation of what happened in the past (to interest and inform): it has also been assumed that most readers wish to be stimulated into thinking further about the topic and to form opinions of their own about the significance of the events that are described and discussed (to be challenged). Thus, although no prior knowledge of the topic is expected on the reader's part, she or he is treated as an intelligent and thinking person throughout. The author tends to share ideas and possibilities with the reader, rather than passing on numbers of so-called 'historical truths'.

To the student reader

Although advantage has been taken of the publication of a second edition to ensure the results of recent research are reflected in the text, the main alteration from the first edition is the inclusion of new features, and the modification of existing ones, aimed at assisting you in your study of the topic at AS level, A level and Higher. Two features are designed to assist you during your first reading of a chapter. The *Points to Consider* section following each chapter title is intended to focus your attention on the main theme(s) of the chapter, and the issues box following most section headings alerts you to the question or questions to be dealt with in the section. The *Working on ...* section at the end of each chapter suggests ways of gaining maximum benefit from the chapter.

There are many ways in which the series can be used by students studying History at a higher level. It will, therefore, be worthwhile thinking about your own study strategy before you start your work on this book. Obviously, your strategy will vary depending on the aim you have in mind, and the time for study that is available to you.

If, for example, you want to acquire a general overview of the topic in the shortest possible time, the following approach will probably be the most effective:

I Read Chapter 1. As you do so, keep in mind the issues raised in the *Points to Consider* section.

2 Read the *Points to Consider* section at the beginning of Chapter 2 and decide whether it is necessary for you to read this chapter.

3 If it is, read the chapter, stopping at each heading or sub-heading to note down the main points that have been made. Often, the best way of doing this is to answer the question(s) posed in the Key Issues boxes.

4 Repeat stage 2 (and stage 3 where appropriate) for all the other chapters.

If, however, your aim is to gain a thorough grasp of the topic, taking however much time is necessary to do so, you may benefit from carrying out the same procedure with each chapter, as follows:

I Try to read the chapter in one sitting. As you do this, bear in mind any advice given in the *Points to Consider* section.

2 Study the flow diagram at the end of the chapter, ensuring that you understand the general 'shape' of what you have just read.

3 Read the *Working on ...* section and decide what further work you need to do on the chapter. In particularly important sections of the book, this is likely to involve reading the chapter a second time and stopping at each heading and sub-heading to think about (and probably to write a summary of) what you have just read.

4 Attempt the *Source-based questions* section. It will sometimes be sufficient to think through your answers, but additional understanding will often be gained by forcing yourself to write them down.

When you have finished the main chapters of the book, study the *Further Reading* section and decide what additional reading (if any) you will do on the topic.

This book has been designed to help make your studies both enjoyable and successful. If you can think of ways in which this could have been done more effectively, please contact us. In the meantime, we hope that you will gain greatly from your study of History.

Keith Randell & Robert Pearce

Acknowledgements

I would like to thank the series editor, Dr Robert Pearce, for the care he has taken in editing this book. His kind, yet rigorous, criticism has certainly made it much better. Thanks also to my colleagues in the History Division at the University of Wolverhampton for all their support, especially to Professor John Benson and Dr Fiona Terry-Chandler who made many helpful suggestions to improve the text and to Dr Malcolm Wanklyn for his encouragement throughout. Both Hilary Bourdillon and Ann Swarbrick helped with the study guides and student exercises, so I would like to thank them too. I am also grateful to the anonymous reader who made many useful detailed suggestions. My greatest thanks are to my husband, Jonathan Dudley, who commented on every chapter and whose support at every level has been appreciated.

The publishers would like to thank the following for permission to reproduce the following copyright illustrations:

Punch Ltd, page 12; Mary Evans Picture Library, page 60; The British Library, page 72; WK Haselden/*Daily Mirror* and for supply of the photograph the Centre for the Study of Cartoons and Caricature, University of Kent, Canterbury, CT2 7NU, page 95; Imperial War Museum, page 111.

The publishers would like to thank the following for permission to reproduce material in the volume:

Indiana University Press for an extract from *Women in England, 1870–1950* by Jane Lewis (1984) used on page 127; Palgrave Macmillan for an extract from *Sylvia Pankhurst* by Barbara Winslow and Sheila Rowbottom (1996) used on page 43; Routledge for an extract from *Before the Vote was Won* by Jane Lewis (1987) used on page 23; Virago Press for an extract from *The Cause* by Ray Strachey (1978) used on page 123.

1 Introduction: Change and Continuity in the Position of Women, 1860–1918

POINTS TO CONSIDER

Votes for Women was clearly a major political issue. However, women also campaigned for other improvements to their lives. This chapter introduces you to the main achievements made by women during this period and, in so doing, places the campaign for the franchise within a wider historical context.

KEY DATES

1857	Divorce Act
1864	The first Contagious Diseases Act
1869	Women able to vote in local elections
1870	Education Act
1870	Married Women's Property Act
1875	First female Poor Law Guardian elected
1878	Domestic science a compulsory subject for girls in Board Schools
1881	Women in the Isle of Man gain the vote
1882	Married Women's Property Act
1884	Matrimonial Causes Act
1885	Criminal Law Amendment Act
1893	First women factory inspectors appointed
1902	Education Act

In 1918 women over the age of 30 who were on the local government register or married to men on the local government register gained the vote, but it was another ten years before women achieved the vote on equal terms with men. Eventually, in 1928, all women, regardless of their marital status or financial position, were enfranchised. Even so, women gained the vote only after a long, and at times highly controversial, campaign. This book tells the story of the suffragists (usually thought of as peaceful campaigners) and the suffragettes (usually thought of as more violent) who fought hard for this objective. Yet, although this book is about women's suffrage, the vote was just one of a number of demands put forward by those who campaigned for social change. By the time women had gained even a limited vote, early feminists (that is women who wanted to improve the position of women) had chalked up some formidable achievements.

1 Education

> **KEY ISSUE** What were the key shifts in educational provision for girls between 1860 and 1928?

Feminists believed that education was the key to unlock the closed doors into the masculine world of politics. In the 1860s, when the campaign for the suffrage began in earnest, the majority of women from all social classes generally lacked a formal education. But by 1918 there had been some remarkable changes, though not all as a response to pressure from women and not always beneficial to them. As Dorothy Thomson has pointed out, generalisations about a whole gender have to be treated with great caution'.[1] Educational developments affected working-class and middle-class girls and women quite differently; and while it is thought to have limited the working class, new educational provision opened up opportunities for their middle-class counterparts.

Until 1870 working-class girls were educated in a variety of ways. Young factory workers attended factory schools, whereas pauper children went to workhouse schools. The remainder of the female population, if formally educated at all, were taught in small fee-paying schools run by older women or in charity schools set up by religious foundations. After 1870 state schools replaced this informal system. The period from 1870 onwards saw the construction of a state education system that by 1918 had made schooling compulsory for all children up to the age of 13. The new state-funded system of education gave some chances for working-class girls to become numerate and literate – by the end of the nineteenth century 97 per cent of all children could read and write – but it offered too narrow a curriculum, too rigid a teaching method and too large a class size to have any great effect on work opportunities for young women. State schools emphasised the domestication, rather than the emancipation, of working-class girls. All too often, the school syllabus included cookery, needlework and housewifery at the expense of other subjects. Indeed, in 1878 domestic economy became a compulsory subject for girls but not for boys. It has been suggested that state schools were more 'finishing schools' for the manual worker rather than educational establishments in any wider sense. By preparing girls either for domestic service or for the role of wife and mother, they reaffirmed, rather than challenged, women's role in society. Change, for the young working-class school girl, did not therefore necessarily mean progress.

In contrast, the changes in middle-class education occurred as a result of pressure from below and, possibly as a consequence of this, offered better opportunities. In mid-nineteenth-century Britain the majority of girls of the middle and upper classes did not go to school but were educated at home by a governess or by a member of their family. Some attended small family-type schools but the nature of their education remained virtually identical to that of those taught at home. Middle-class and upper-class girls were educated to be wives and mothers of men from the same social class as themselves. It was unthinkable that they would go out to work for a living. By 1918, largely through the combined efforts of feminists and the government, this situation had changed to some extent because a number of new schools, which offered an academic curriculum consisting of science, economics and mathematics, were opened for the daughters of middle- and upper-class families.

Feminists also worked hard to achieve access for women into higher education. By 1860 both Queen's and Bedford College, in London, had educated a number of leading feminists (such as Barbara Bodichon and Elizabeth Blackwell), yet the rest of higher education remained resolutely male. All women, whatever their intelligence or capability, were denied access to both universities and medical schools. This prompted a number of feminists to campaign for women to be admitted to medical training and into the universities. They also promoted the training of teachers. By the end of the nineteenth century both London and Manchester Universities accepted women, various women's colleges had been founded at Oxford and Cambridge (even though women were not allowed to be awarded degrees) and women's teacher training colleges were established. In turn these women went to teach in the newly opened secondary schools for girls. However, despite the opening of a Working Women's College in London in the 1860s, opportunities for working-class women remained limited. Furthermore, with an increasing emphasis placed on teacher training, the old pupil-teacher scheme (whereby bright working-class girls learnt to become teachers by working in a classroom alongside a fully qualified professional) fell into disrepute and was soon abandoned.

2 Work

> **KEY ISSUE** To what extent did women's expectations of work change over this period?

As with education, there were great differences in the working patterns of middle-class and working-class women. Indeed, there were two labour markets for women in this period: one for working-class women and another for the middle class. Apart from a brief interlude during the First World War, domestic service continued to be the most common occupation for working-class women: one in three such were domestic servants at some time in their lives.

Cotton was Britain's most important export throughout this time, so it is not surprising that textile work remained the second most important job for women. However, this work was concentrated in the cotton towns of northern England and in parts of Scotland. In the rest of the British Isles women were employed in a variety of unskilled and low paid jobs. Yet there were a number of new developments. The growth of banking and commerce, and the subsequent inventions of the typewriter and the telephone, created new opportunities for the 'white blouse' worker as she was known. Nevertheless, despite a number of trade union and government attempts to improve wages and working conditions, working-class women remained at the bottom of the economic scale. Equality with men was a long way off as most women workers continued to earn about 65 per cent of a male wage.

On the other hand, when this book begins, it was expected that middle-class women – single or married – should remain at home, look after their families and engage in charitable works. If they were forced to work for payment, as many were, the occupation of governess was open to them. By 1914, however, middle-class women had created new professions and had made a few inroads into a number of previously male dominated ones. A School for Nursing, for instance, was established at St Thomas's Hospital, London, in 1860 by Florence Nightingale which attracted middle-class women. Women also gained the right to become doctors, architects, factory and workhouse inspectors and to enter the civil service. By far the greatest number, however, became teachers. Even so, there were still a number of professions, such as the law, banking and the stock exchange, which remained closed to women. Until the First World War, the sexual division of labour, whereby women and men were designated to do different jobs, remained almost insuperable. During this war, which lasted from 1914 to 1918, the nature of women's work altered dramatically. But this turned out to be a temporary measure since most women returned to their traditional jobs when the war ended.

3 Marriage

> **KEY ISSUE** What were the main obstacles preventing women from achieving marital equality in this period?

Pressure from feminists was largely responsible for persuading Parliament to make a number of significant changes in the legal position of both working-class and middle-class married women in the nineteenth and early twentieth centuries. When the suffrage movement began, women very much remained the unequal partner in marriage, so not surprisingly feminists of the time campaigned to end a number of the grosser legal injustices. Some of the areas of concern centred on property rights, marital rights, custody of children and divorce. For example, once married, women were considered the property of their husbands: husbands owned the home and the wealth of their wives, whether or not they were still living together. In the notorious case of the Norton family, George Norton took all the money earned by his wife Caroline after they had separated. On the other hand, husbands were responsible for their wives' debts and so, in return, Caroline Norton ran up bills which her husband was forced to pay. After considerable campaigning by feminists – such as the suffragist and suffragette Elizabeth Wolstenholme Elmy – the Married Women's Property Acts of 1870 and 1882 gave, if not equal status to women, then a stepping stone to future reform.

There were other improvements too. The Matrimonial Causes Act in 1884 went some way towards ending marital injustice by denying husbands the right to lock up their wives because they refused to have sex with them. In 1891 this Act was reinforced by the Court of Appeal which upheld a complaint by women campaigners on behalf of a Mrs Jackson, who had been locked up by her husband. Mrs Jackson had refused to live with Mr Jackson so he had grabbed his wife outside her church in Clitheroe, forced her into his carriage, took her to his home and locked her up. Fortunately for Mrs Jackson, her friends led a campaign for her release and after a long legal struggle the Court of Appeal decided that Mr Jackson had no statutory right to force his wife to live with him. Mrs Jackson may have won her case but she suffered from considerable hostility from the people in her home town for refusing to live with her husband. Moreover, despite the efforts of a number of feminists, wife-battering and marital rape remained legal.

Divorce law exhibited similar inequalities. Before 1857 it was extremely difficult and very expensive to obtain a divorce in England. Only very rich – and determined – men were generally able to afford the high costs of divorce. The 1857 Divorce Act reformed the divorce law but it benefited men rather than women. Men were able to divorce their wives for adultery, whereas women had to prove either bigamy, rape, sodomy, bestiality, cruelty or long-term desertion to gain a divorce. This, argued nineteenth-century feminists, consolidated the sexual double standard (the moral standard whereby it was acceptable for men, but not women, to have sex outside marriage) because it laid down different grounds for divorce. Moreover, once divorced, women found it difficult to obtain maintenance and custody of their children. There were some improvements in the 1870s and 1880s: wives who had been beaten or deserted by their husbands were granted maintenance and divorced women were given some custody rights over their children. Nevertheless marital equality with men was not achieved by the time women won the vote.

4 Sexual Morality

> **KEY ISSUE** To what extent was the challenge to the sexual double standard successful?

In this period a number of women were dismayed by the sexual double standard whereby women had to remain virginal before marriage and faithful inside it. On the other hand, a blind eye was turned if men had sex with more than one partner. One of women's greatest victories was the repeal of the Contagious Diseases Acts (CDAs) in 1886. These Acts, the first of which had been passed in 1864, allowed police in a number of garrison towns and naval ports the right to arrest women suspected of being common prostitutes and require them to be medically examined for venereal disease. If found infected, women could be detained for treatment. This, according to feminists, was unfair because it blamed prostitutes for the spread of venereal disease not the men who used their services. Under the leadership of Josephine Butler, the Ladies' National Association led a campaign to repeal these Acts and eventually succeeded 22 years after they had been passed.

The success of this campaign prompted feminists to launch a crusade against the sexual exploitation of young girls. In 1885 they achieved a victory when the Criminal Law Amendment Act, which raised the age of sexual consent to 16, was passed. Feminists and others founded the National Vigilance Association to ensure that this Act was put into practice and to promote equal high moral standards amongst the sexes. Edwardian feminists, such as Christabel Pankhurst, took up the social purity cause and demanded that men improve their moral code by remaining chaste outside marriage. Although feminists achieved a small victory in repealing the CDAs, the campaign to raise moral standards can be considered to have failed miserably.

5 Politics

> **KEY ISSUE** What opportunities existed for women in politics at this time?

Women may not have achieved the British Parliamentary vote until 1918 but there were other political achievements. On 1 January 1881, 700 British women were able to vote at the House of Keys in the Isle of Man, 37 years before women in mainland Britain were granted the same privilege. The Manx, as the people who live in the Isle of Man are known, had kept their own institutions, independent of Britain, and governed themselves through the Tynwald Court, which had an Upper Chamber and an elected House of Keys.

Elsewhere in Britain, women were engaged in politics through their party organisations. The Women's Liberal Federation, which was founded in 1886, was an autonomous, women-only organisation that offered invaluable training to feminists. Delegates at Annual meetings claimed the right to define party policy and concerned themselves with suffrage and with radical social policies, such as health, housing and education. Similarly the Independent Labour Party, founded in 1893, attracted large numbers of women activists who spoke at meetings, wrote articles in newspapers and helped develop party policy. Women also joined the women's section of the Conservative Party but tended to play more of a secondary role than their Liberal and Labour counterparts.

It is sometimes forgotten that some women achieved the vote in local government long before they won the right to vote in national elections. In 1869 single or widowed rate-paying women were given the right to vote for municipal councils and the later county councils; in 1907 all women rate-payers were allowed to vote in local government elections. Middle-class women in London's poorest areas 'worked all hours to get property repaired and fumigated, drains rebuilt, infant mortality reduced, and open spaces inserted into the slums'.[2] Women also encouraged authorities to build public lavatories, baths and parks for the inhabitants of working-class districts. However, after the Liberals swept into power in 1906, electors began to vote Tory in town councils and so large numbers of women – who tended to be left-wing – lost their seats.

In 1870, as a result of the Education Act, women were eligible to serve on the newly created School Boards. These School Boards had responsibility for the education of children in state schools from the age of five upwards. Some women sought election because they wanted to make a public statement that women were capable of governing. Others, such as the suffragist Lydia Becker, tried to put their feminist ideas into practice by encouraging boys as well as girls to do cooking and needlework. However, when Local Education Authorities replaced School Boards in 1902, women were declared ineligible for election.

In 1875 the first woman Poor Law Guardian was elected and by 1900 there were approximately 1000 women Guardians, many of whom, like Emmeline Pankhurst, tried to mitigate the worst excesses of workhouse life. As a Poor Law Guardian in Manchester, she found

1   old folks sitting on backless forms or benches. They had no privacy, no possessions, not even a locker. The old women were without pockets in their gowns so they were obliged to keep any poor little treasures they had in their bosoms. Soon after I took office we gave the old
5   people comfortable Windsor chairs to sit in, and in a number of ways we managed to make their existence more endurable.[3]

Agatha Stacey, a Birmingham Poor Law Guardian, was so concerned about the poor in the local workhouse that she helped to found homes for the homeless, single mothers and the mentally retarded. A number of female Poor Law Guardians were prominent figures in Poor Law administration nationally and used their influence to initiate reforms elsewhere.

Women who campaigned for social change faced heavy criticism because they criticised the 'separate spheres' philosophy. According to Victorian and Edwardian sentiment, God made men and women biologically different, and so it made sense that they performed distinct roles. Women were the only sex able to become pregnant, have babies and breast-feed, so it was thought appropriate for them to remain within the 'private sphere' of the home. Not surprisingly, women were also believed to be better qualified for the domestic jobs of cooking, cleaning and child-rearing because home was their natural domain. In contrast, men's historic hunting role made them innately suited to the 'public sphere' of work and politics. In claiming a share of the 'public sphere' for women, feminists therefore challenged the fundamental principles of society.

During the period 1860 to 1918 women experienced a number of significant improvements to their lives. However, blatant inequalities remained and it was these that stirred the campaigning spirits of the suffragists and the suffragettes. And so, by the time Edward VII became King in 1901, the vote had become their major focus of attention.

References

1 Dorothy Thompson in *Equal or Different*, Jane Rendall (Basil Blackwell, 1987), p. 71.
2 Patricia Hollis in *Equal or Different*, Jane Rendall (Basil Blackwell, 1987), p. 204.
3 *My Own Story*, Emmeline Pankhurst (Virago, 1979), p. 24.

Summary Diagram
Change and Continuity in the Position of Women 1860–1918

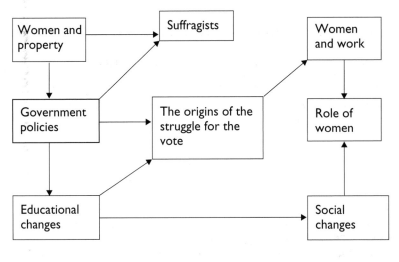

Having read this chapter, you should be familiar with the structure of British society in the period 1860–1918 and the position of women in this. Although you are unlikely to be asked a direct question on this period, knowledge of it is useful in understanding the background to the suffrage struggle. You may well find it useful to make notes on:

- The main problems faced by women before 1902
- The impact of campaigns for social and legal change by women.

Consider the following question:

a) Describe the main problems facing women in the years 1860–1902. (*15 marks*)
b) What measures were taken to meet the demands by women for social reform in Britain in the years 1857–1902? (*15 marks*)

With questions of this nature you will need to be aware of the key demands made by women from different sectors of society and how governments responded to them. It would be useful to outline three or four major factors, develop their significance and make judgements based on the evidence presented in this chapter. Remember to keep referring to the question when constructing your answer.

2 Votes for Women: The Debate

POINTS TO CONSIDER

It is sometimes supposed that campaigners for votes for women regarded the vote as an end in itself. This is not so. Both suffragists (those who engaged in peaceful campaigning) and suffragettes (those who engaged in violent actions) wanted the vote to end women's economic and social subordination and to brighten their future lives. Many disagreed with women's suffrage. Your aim in this chapter is to understand the main arguments of both those who supported and opposed votes for women and to account for the similarities and differences between them.

KEY DATES

1832   Great Reform Bill
1867   Second Reform Bill
1872   Secret Ballot
1883   Corrupt Practices Act
1884   Third Reform Bill

Votes for Women created a great deal of discussion. Not surprisingly, given the broad political composition of the suffrage movement, there emerged several different arguments in support of votes for women. Moreover the debate changed over time as new ideas emerged about the role of women in British life. Historians have viewed these arguments in a number of ways. Constitutional historians tend to stress the political reasons why women sought the vote; socialist feminists tend to emphasise the economic causes; and radical feminists tend to concentrate on the part that sexual politics played. However, some of the latest research suggests that beliefs in British, and sometimes white, superiority underpinned the women's suffrage campaign. Certainly, fears were expressed that black men were gaining the vote elsewhere whereas white women were still excluded.

Those who opposed women's suffrage (the Antis) marshalled equally numerous arguments against votes for women. At first the Antis found it easy to discredit women's suffrage by commenting on the psychological differences between the sexes and the inappropriateness of women taking part in politics. Over the years they were forced to sharpen up their arguments as those in favour of the female franchise refuted each of their objections and as public opinion changed. Until recently historians have generally ignored this opposition movement possibly because it was considered unfashionable – and perhaps politically incorrect – to examine those who were hostile to what is now considered a perfectly reasonable demand.

1 The Case for Votes for Women

> **KEY ISSUE** What were the main arguments in support of votes for women?

a) The Rights of Women

Historians agree that early suffragists claimed what they believed to be the restoration of an old right rather than the exercise of a new privilege. Suffragists argued that women had in the past played a significant role in parliamentary politics and drew on many historical examples to support their claim. Abbesses, they argued, had owned vast tracts of land in the medieval period and attended and participated in the early Parliaments. In particular, the abbesses of Barking and Winchester, who headed two of the most prestigious abbeys in medieval England, had been involved in policy-making at the highest level. Even when the English Reformation (by closing abbeys and convents) put paid to religious women's formal involvement in Parliamentary affairs, lay women continued to influence politics. In the sixteenth century, suffragists insisted, women freeholders were still able to vote at parliamentary elections. In 1867 large numbers of women householders re-claimed this old privilege and tried to register. Despite the fact that many successfully placed themselves on the electoral roll, most were rejected. This led to an appeal in the Court of Common Pleas where over 5000 Manchester women, defended by Richard Pankhurst, claimed the right to vote. The judges disagreed with this claim and held that 'every woman is personally incapable' of voting. And so, after 1868, because the suffragists lost the legal case for women's suffrage, the argument that women were legally entitled to vote also lost its persuasive appeal.

Since manhood suffrage was based on property qualifications, both suffragists and suffragettes thought it particularly inequitable that women were denied the vote. This argument gained considerable ground after each extension of the franchise gave the vote to more and more men on the basis of property. When the property qualification for the male vote was lowered in 1867 and again in 1884, more and more wealthy women saw men less well-off than themselves obtain the vote. Although some women owned and controlled vast acres of land, enjoyed fortunes derived from industry and were both householders and taxpayers, they did not have equal privileges with men of their class as they were unable to take part in the fundamental process of democracy. After 1884 30,000 Englishwomen farmers watched many of their male agricultural workers use their newly acquired vote while they remained disenfranchised. It was therefore argued that as women were permitted to hold property, they should be permitted to exercise the political rights that possession of

THE DIGNITY OF THE FRANCHISE.

QUALIFIED VOTER. "AH, YOU MAY PAY RATES AN' TAXES, AN' YOU MAY 'AVE RESPONSERBILITIES AN' ALL; BUT WHEN IT COMES TO *VOTIN'*, YOU MUST LEAVE IT TO *US MEN!*"

Punch cartoon reproduced by the Women's Social and Political Union (WSPU).

property brought to its holder. The cartoon shown on page 12 illustrates this well. It was first produced by *Punch*, a satirical magazine, but was later used by the WSPU as propaganda in support of votes for women. The man entering the polling station is obviously working-class and is portrayed, by both his physical appearance, his body language and his speech, as inferior to the upright, respectable and middle-class woman left outside. This cartoon confirmed the women's suffrage argument that illiterate and uneducated men were enfranchised, and probably shouldn't have been, whereas educated and literate women were denied the vote. Furthermore taxation and representation were seen to be inextricably linked in the British parliamentary system as it was held that those who put money into the national purse should be able to control its spending. From at least the 1860s onwards those who campaigned for women's suffrage complained that even when women paid taxes they had no control over how those taxes were spent. In 1910 a Women's Tax Resistance League was set up as a channel for the bitterness these women felt.

Historians have frequently seen the issue of the vote as the last in a set of other economic, social and political rights. David Morgan, for example, places the campaign for the vote within the wider and more general context of female emancipation. By the end of the nineteenth century, Morgan argues, women had obtained most of the benefits that a political democracy could afford: they were enjoying improved educational opportunities; they were permeating the technological and professional labour market; and they were increasingly joining trade unions to campaign for their economic rights. Certainly, suffragists drew attention to the increasing gap between women's economic participation and their continual absence from the political sphere. However, it is important to remember that the campaigns for the vote took place at the same time, rather than after, the campaigns for legal changes and other rights. In addition, as the introduction to this book has demonstrated, success in these areas was limited. The campaign for the vote should therefore be seen as part and parcel of the women's movement of the nineteenth and early twentieth centuries not just the last emancipatory hurdle to be overcome.

b) Growth of Democracy

The vote is also said by historians to have had an important symbolic significance: it was the hallmark of citizenship in a country governed by a representative institution. Suffragists were therefore disheartened when women were consistently omitted from each of the franchise reform Acts of 1832, 1867 and 1884 and were thus denied full citizenship status. The Great Reform Act of 1832 swept away many of the abuses of the Parliamentary system but the new vote was confined merely to men with property. Suffragists argued that, for the first time in legal and political history, women were explicitly excluded from participating in the democratic process because those who framed the Act had deliberately used the term 'male' rather than 'persons'. The attainment of household suffrage in the boroughs in 1867 threw the exclusion of women from the democratic process into even sharper relief. Although not all men were enfranchised – the residence qualification meant that domestic servants, the armed forces and sons living at home were still excluded – many were. By 1884 two-thirds of adult males had gained the vote, but to all women, as to criminals and to patients in lunatic asylums, it was denied. Suffragists considered it inappropriate to claim that Britain had a representative government when the majority of the population was disenfranchised on the grounds of gender. They argued that no government, least of all one that saw itself as democratic, should want to preside over what was essentially an undemocratic system. By the end of the nineteenth century Britain's politics were criticised for being both unjust and unbalanced.

The successful participation of a small number of women in both party and local politics reinforced women's claim to the parliamentary vote. The three franchise reform Acts of the nineteenth century, combined with the secret ballot of 1872 and the Corrupt Practices Act of 1883 (which limited the use of paid canvassers), created a need for sophisticated party machines to organise the new mass electorate. Various women's organisations were set up within the main parties with the dual purpose of shaping women's opinion and canvassing votes. Women also made a significant contribution to local politics and to philanthropy. If women helped men get elected then it appeared illogical for them not to be able to vote themselves. Since 1869 single women and widowed rate-payers were able to vote in municipal elections, and once again it seemed absurd for them to be denied the parliamentary vote. Women also made a significant contribution to local politics by helping to clean up the towns, by helping provide better education and by improving the lives of paupers in workhouses. The accomplishments of women in party and local politics made it abundantly clear to suffragists that they were fit to be entrusted with the vote. Moreover, as much of education and Poor Law legislation was centrally directed it seemed to be an odd perversity that women laboured under laws they had not helped to frame. It was considered unfair that a few distinguished women, who had already made a significant contribution to the country's good, should be disenfranchised while illiterate and uneducated men were free to vote. Women such as Louisa Twining (workhouse reformer), Angela Burdett-Coutts (famous rich philanthropist) and Florence Nightingale (nursing reformer) were cited by suffragists as examples of women who had advanced the cause of reform politics and who would contribute much of value – for both men and women – to future parliaments.

Suffragists, and later suffragettes, pointed to the fact that a number of countries had enfranchised their female population – the Isle of Man in 1881, New Zealand in 1893, Finland in 1906, Norway in 1907, various states in Australia between 1893 and 1909 and a number of American States – without calamitous results. British suffragists used these successes to demonstrate that British women should be enfranchised too. They argued that votes for women elsewhere cast a shadow on the country that was supposedly the 'mother of democracy'. It had been presumed that Britain would lead other nations in enfranchising women and the fact that other countries had done so challenged British democratic supremacy. British suffragists also claimed that votes for women in the various American states had brought about a reform in political organisations and led to a calm and orderly election process. The granting of the vote to all women in the Isle of Man, Australia and New Zealand was especially significant since these three countries shared a similar social and political culture. With their respectably high turn-out at the polls, both Australia and New Zealand corroborated suffrage arguments that women wanted the vote even if they did not campaign actively for it. In addition they illustrated that women would exercise the vote responsibly and demonstrated, as with the USA, that women would clean up political life. These successes were encouraging for British suffragists since it gave them positive signals that theirs was not a lone struggle against unbelievable odds.

c) Means to an End

Of course, it was not just the vote as a symbol of citizenship that mattered but the use to which it could be put. At the beginning of the nineteenth century the vote had been less significant than patronage in Parliamentary politics and, with so many of the population denied the vote, it had little real influence on government thinking. However, historians suggest that by the end of the nineteenth century suffragists believed that under a representative government, the interests of any non-represented group were liable to be neglected. The group that held political power, which was men, made laws favourable to themselves and neglected the interests of those without power, including women. This reasoning was borne out by experience: as more and more men were enfranchised, so laws were enacted that reflected the wishes of the various classes of male voter. After 1832 the Whigs passed a series of laws including the Poor Law Amendment Act (1834) that represented the particular interests of the newly enfranchised middle-class male, whereas after 1867, when working-class men were granted the vote, important educational and trade union reforms were introduced. In contrast, it was believed that women faced hardship because their views remained unrepresented. As J S Mill pointed out, 'women do not need political rights in order that they may govern, but in order that they may not be misgoverned'.[1] Indeed the male electorate was seen to use their sole power to make laws, such as the Contagious Diseases Acts (see page 6), which adversely affected, and were strongly resented by, women. Moreover, whereas early Victorian governments adhered much more to the principle of *laissez faire*, it was apparent by the Edwardian era that this principle was dead and that Parliament, as the governing body of the country, had power to change the way people worked and lived

Once women had obtained the vote, suffragists and suffragettes argued, governments would be forced to take women's issues seriously. Both groups considered the vote to be a defence against the tyranny of men over women and believed that when women were enfranchised their oppression would end. But even though the vote was seen as a means to the end of greater social justice, that end varied considerably. For some it meant economic reform and the improvement of women's financial situation; for another group it meant legal reform and the improvement of women's marital position; while for others it meant social reform and the improvement of women's condition more generally.

Socialist feminist historians such as Liddington and Norris tend to focus on the fact that suffragists wanted the vote to improve the pay, conditions and lives of working women. In 1872 suffragists alleged that, in England alone, nearly 3 million unmarried women and 800,000 married women received wages far below those of men of the same class. Forty years later, suffragettes were making similar complaints. In 1912 it was believed that male working-class wages had risen throughout the late nineteenth and early twentieth centuries because men were able, through their trade unions, to pressurise Parliament into passing laws favourable to them. In contrast, it was believed that women's trade unions accomplished less, largely because they were without the vote. Women not only earned less than half the male wage but were barred from a number of occupations. Throughout the nineteenth century governments had excluded women from certain types of work, restricted their hours and regulated their working conditions. For example, women had been banned from working underground in coal mines in 1842, while in 1844 they had had their hours restricted in textile factories. Many suffragists objected to this 'protective' legislation because it either deprived women of jobs or made them compete unfairly with men for work, resulting in the further lowering of female wages and, paradoxically, in women being dismissed in favour of men. In the Edwardian period, suffragettes put forward similar arguments and believed that the vote would help to bring about economic equality between men and women.

Throughout the nineteenth century suffragists wanted the vote as a legal protection against avaricious and cruel husbands. Before the

Married Women's Property Acts were passed (1870 and 1882) the common law deprived women of the right to keep their own property and money. Even after 1882 the British marriage laws were considered the most barbarous in Europe as husbands still had the right to beat their wives and compel them to return if they left home. Children over seven were legally the property of their fathers, who were able to take them away from their mothers if they wished. By the beginning of the twentieth century, when many legal injustices had been removed, both suffragists and suffragettes turned to issues of sex and morality.

Until the recent work of feminist historians most history texts ignored the emphasis placed on sex and morality by the suffragists and suffragettes. The few historians who do mention it have often used it as an excuse to ridicule the suffragettes. In particular, George Dangerfield and Roger Fulford both dismiss the WSPU's cry for 'Votes for Women' and 'Chastity for Men' as an amusing peculiarity, while Rosen discounts such slogans as examples of spinsterish eccentricity. However, the relationship between sexuality and the vote has enjoyed a long history in the annals of women's suffrage. Both the suffragists and the suffragettes positioned women's franchise within the wider context of sexual politics and took the question of sexuality very earnestly indeed. For some suffrage campaigners such as Millicent Fawcett and Christabel Pankhurst the vote was as much about improving men's sexual morality as it was about improving women's working conditions.

The majority of suffragists remained opposed to debates about female sexuality, fearing that it would offend Victorian prudery and so lessen support for the cause. But a number wanted the vote to cleanse the perceived corruption in public life by ensuring that men and women adhered to the same moral principles. This, they believed, would go some way towards eliminating venereal disease. In this sense, the women's suffrage movement was seen as much as a moral movement as a political one. Indeed, some suffragists believed in a female moral superiority, whereby women were the keepers of virtue and men the lustful destroyers of chastity. Lydia Becker, one of the founders of the suffragist movement, insisted that the vote was 'a protection for women from the uncontrolled dominion of the savage passions of men.' Over 30 years later, Emmeline Pankhurst confidently assumed that votes for women were necessary to eliminate the sexual double standard whereby it was acceptable for men, but not women, to engage in pre-marital sex. When Emmeline Pankhurst was a Poor Law Guardian she had been distressed by the increasing number of single mothers who were dependent on the state because men refused to marry them or pay them maintenance. Throughout her life, she constantly made references to the abhorrent selfishness in male sexual activity. Her daughter Christabel even claimed that venereal disease (she claimed 75 per cent of men were infected with gonorrhea and 25 per cent with syphilis!) would be eliminated once women had the vote. In her pamphlet *The Great Scourge* she argued that the subjection of women was the fundamental cause of venereal disease and promoted a two-fold political programme of chastity for men and votes for women. Indeed, she fervently believed that once women were enfranchised laws could be passed to transform male sexual behaviour:

1 the canker of venereal disease is eating away the vitals of the nation, and the only cure is Votes for Women. ... The real cure of the great plague is – Votes for Women, which will give to women more self-reliance and a stronger economic position and chastity for men ... Apart from the
5 deplorable moral effect of the fact that women are voteless, there is this to be noticed – that the law of the land, as made and administered by men, protects and encourages the immorality of men, and the sex exploitation of women.[2]

This extract from her pamphlet, which might read a little strangely to modern eyes, needs to be placed within historical context. People in Victorian and Edwardian Britain were anxious about the increase of venereal disease and its far reaching effects not only on the health of the individual but on that of the nation. Nevertheless, it is fair to argue that Christabel Pankhurst cherished too many assumptions about the superiority of female virtue and expressed a minority view when she associated venereal disease with votes for women.

The vote was also seen as a device that could be utilised to curb unfair legislation against prostitutes and ultimately to end prostitution. In particular, Victorian suffragists were critical of the Contagious Diseases Acts (CDAs) of the 1860s because they blamed prostitutes for venereal disease, not the men who paid for their services. Feminists, under the leadership of Josephine Butler's Ladies' National Association (LNA), opposed these Acts and supported votes for women to end this legal injustice. Meanwhile, because they believed the CDAs to be so unfair, the membership of the LNA continued to campaign against them in the hope that an all-male Parliament might repeal the Acts. Some went even further. Millicent Fawcett not only supported the LNA campaigns but believed that the vote would also end prostitution. As President of both the National Union of Women's Suffrage Societies (NUWSS) and the National Union of Women Workers (an umbrella organisation initially concerned with the elimination of prostitution), Fawcett was well placed to see a direct connection between women's lack of franchise and the existence of prostitution. This link was also confirmed by a leading member of the NUWSS in the early years of the twentieth century:

1 We wish for it [the vote] because there exists a terrible trade of procuring young girls for immoral purposes. The girl is first entrapped and seduced, and when once she has fallen, it is very difficult for her to return afterwards to her home, or to be received among respectable
5 girls in workshops or in domestic service. She becomes a prostitute ... we believe the time has come when women must claim their right to

help ... and the first step to this lies in their enfranchisement, for without this they have no real power in the matter. It would be much more
difficult for this cruel and wicked traffic to be carried on if it were
10 recognised by the law that women were of the same value and had the
same standing in the State as men.

The causes of prostitution were located within the economic and political context of dependency: most women did not earn enough to support
themselves and relied too much on men to help them out. Christabel
Pankhurst went further and argued that prostitution was based on male
vice, which could only be eradicated when women had the vote.

More recently historians place the reasons why women wanted the
vote within the context of British imperialism. They argue that 'a
sense of national and racial superiority based on Britain's imperial
status was an organising principle of Victorian culture'[3] and that most
feminists subscribed to the belief that the Anglo-Saxon race was
superior to all others. Many Quaker suffragists initially made comparisons between women's rights and the abolition of slavery by supporting the emancipation of both women and black people. But by
the end of the nineteenth century a number of suffragists had
changed their minds. They feared that when black males in the
United States were enfranchised in the 1860s it sent out the racial
message that black men were capable of exercising political judgement whereas the majority of the white race – that is women – were
not. As a result, they thought it imperative to grant the vote to British
women in order to safeguard white supremacy. Furthermore, many
suffrage workers assumed that Britain was in a more advanced state of
social development than people of other countries. The following
extract from a speech made by the MP Clive Eastwick in the debate in
the House of Commons on the Women's Disabilities Bill on 3 May
1871 indicates that these ideas of racial superiority were widely held.

1 There was a special reason why this country should be the first to
adopt the enfranchisement of women. That reason was the immense
influence which the example of England must exert upon the 200 millions of Asiatics in India, among whom, with a few brilliant exceptions,
5 women have been degraded to a state little better than slavery. How
could we expect that Indian women would be emancipated from the
imprisonment of the zenanah [harem] or be admitted to the full privileges of education, so long as we continued to proclaim the inferiority
of women in this country?

Over 30 years later, the leadership of the WSPU reiterated this. In an
editorial for *Votes for Women*, Christabel Pankhurst argued that British
women were the rightful heirs to democracy. She felt it was disgrace-
ful that 'they should have their inheritance withheld, while men of
other races are suddenly and almost without preparation leaping into
possession of constitutional power' According to one historian, both
suffragists and suffragettes advocated the vote for white women over

black men because Britain, as the Mother of Parliaments, provided a role model that other countries should emulate rather than the other way round. However, the emphasis on the relationship between women's suffrage, imperialism, and sometimes racism perhaps rests more on historical interpretation than actuality. Both the NUWSS and the WSPU constantly emphasised the need for women all over the world to unite in their campaign for the vote. Indeed the WSPU made it clear that for their members the unity of women overrode differences in colour, race or creed.

Radical though some of these sentiments were, neither the suffragists nor the suffragettes wanted the vote as a way of undermining women's role in the home. Indeed, all sides reiterated their commitment to the separate spheres philosophy whereby women and men held distinct roles within society. In their view, democracy needed a woman's touch. Millicent Fawcett held that women 'wanted the home-side represented in politics ... woman at her best stood for mercy, pity, peace, purity and love'.[4] As Sandra Holton has pointed out, suffrage activists believed women to have the necessary mothering qualities needed for a state increasingly committed to social reform and improving the lives of its citizens.

Clearly women wanted the vote for a number of different reasons. Evidence for this can be seen in the following extract:

Why Women Want the Vote

1 **BECAUSE** no race or class or sex can have its interest properly safeguarded in the legislature of a country unless it is represented by direct suffrage.

BECAUSE while men who are voters can get their economic
5 grievances listened to, non-voters are disregarded.

BECAUSE politics and economics go hand in hand. And so long as woman has no political status she will be the 'bottom dog' as a wage-earner.

BECAUSE the Legislature in the past has not made laws which
10 are equal between men and women: and these laws will not be altered till women get the vote.

BECAUSE all the more important and lucrative positions are barred to them, and opportunities of public service are denied.

BECAUSE wherever women have become voters, reform has
15 proceeded more rapidly than before, and even at home our municipal government, in which the women have a certain share, is in advance and not behind our Parliamentary attitude on many important questions.

BECAUSE women will be better comrades to their husbands,
20 better mothers to their children, and better housekeepers of the home.

---

2 The Case Against Votes for Women

> **KEY ISSUES** What were the main arguments of those who were opposed to votes for women? How did these compare with the arguments put forward by suffragists?

To most of us in the twenty-first century the ideas of the opponents of women's suffrage, often called the Antis, may seem wildly unconvincing. But we have to remember that, at the time, these ideas were more representative of popular opinion than those of the female suffragists. It is also important to remember that the Antis were not all men: a number of eminent women (such as Mary Kingsley and Gertrude Bell, distinguished Victorian and Edwardian explorers) spoke out against votes for women. The Antis' arguments were varied but generally centred on the perceived physical, emotional and intellectual differences between men and women. As Frederick Pethick-Lawrence, a strong supporter of women's suffrage, remarked about the Antis,

1 Men, it was said, were governed by reason, women by emotion. If once the franchise were thrown open to women, they would ... force an emotional policy on the country ... In particular it was said that on sex matters women were narrower and harder than men; and that if they
5 were given power they would impose impossibly strict standards of morality ... A further fear was that women ... would lose their special charm and attraction. A slightly different motive was the innate love of domination. This was sometimes expressed in the blunt rejoinder: 'Votes for Women', indeed: we shall be asked next to give votes to our
10 horses and dogs.[5]

a) The Right to Rule

As Brian Harrison has pointed out, those opposed to votes for women were often people with an inherent dislike of change and with no wish to alter the political status quo. To their minds, any extension of the franchise, either male or female, would have deleterious effects on the country because it would destabilise the existing political structure. A few Antis were opposed to any increase in democracy because they feared that an 'uneducated, politically inexperienced and irrational class'[6] would gain ascendancy over the body politic. Indeed, opponents of women's suffrage believed that a small political elite (i.e. themselves) were destined to – and should – rule over the mass of the population. For a lot of Antis it was self-evident that women should not vote simply because they were women. At first, Harrison argues, the inferiority of women seemed so obvious that it needed no further explanation, but gradually the Antis claimed an intellectual basis for their views.

Many Antis stressed the relationship between the right to vote and the responsibility to fight for one's country. Women, it was alleged, were not capable of full citizenship because they were not available for the defence of the realm. One female leading anti-suffragist argued that women should not have the vote because political power, exercised either overseas or domestically, rested in the end on physical force to which women, owing to physical, moral and social reasons, were not capable of contributing. This argument against votes for women remained remarkably consistent between 1860 and 1914 but it was one that had several strands. The first strand rested on Britain's role as an imperial power. Antis argued that since Britain ruled a vast empire she needed a strong army. No country with imperial pretensions offered female suffrage, they said, because women could not fight; and because women could never fulfil this vital obligation of citizenship, they should be denied the right to vote. In addition many believed that countries, such as India, over which Britain ruled would not give British authority the same respect if she were governed by women (the fact that Queen Victoria was head of state seemed not to bother them). It was also feared that colonised countries would demand their own enfranchisement, which would inevitably lead to demands for independence.

The second strand rested on fears that women's enfranchisement would introduce a new era of pacifism, as women would be reluctant to wage wars against foreign enemies. As a consequence Britain might go into decline and face invasion because women generally favoured peace rather than war. Concern was particularly expressed that the ever strengthening economic and military position of a masculinised Germany could quickly subdue an increasingly femininised Britain. The third strand rested on the belief that domestic political power needed a show of armed strength to support it. Women would be unable to govern because of their inability to enforce the laws they had made; this would inevitably lead to anarchy, a brutal civil war and ultimately the end of British civilisation.

b) Psychological Differences

Men and women were perceived, by the Antis, as very different from each other not only physically but psychologically and intellectually. Victorian scientific theory legitimised this belief by suggesting that the differences rested on a biological basis. Women were seen to be intellectually inferior to men because their brains weighed less on a set of measuring scales. Moreover, medical opinion claimed that women were guided by their wombs – which were seen to be particularly unstable at puberty, menstruation, pregnancy and menopause –

rather than by their brains. It followed that women were more prone to insanity. 'The point of hysterical emotion and unreason is always nearer with women ... their nerve force is slighter, their self-restraint less.'[7] Indeed the word hysteria is derived from the Greek word for womb. Women, at the mercy of their reproductive cycle, were seen as fickle, childish, capricious and bad-tempered, making it easy for Antis to argue that women were unlikely to make rational judgements about political issues or events. In a House of Commons debate on women's suffrage in 1871, one MP commented that because reason predominated in the man and emotion in the woman it was foolish to grant votes for women: it would mean a House of Commons dominated by sentiment at the expense of logic. Generally, Antis dwelt on the defects of temperament and intellect of women and argued that, as women were likely to regard politics in personal terms, they would become absorbed with the trivial and the domestic rather than with the more important high politics.

Antis also believed that it was God's wish that men should rule and women be governed. Biblical references to Adam and Eve were made: Eve was formed from the spare rib of Adam and so was subject to his rule. The sexes, it was argued, occupied two separate spheres, and politics was very much part of the public sphere belonging to men. For after all, it was the responsibility of the male head of household to defend his family, to go out to work and to run the political system. Mrs Humphrey Ward, a famous novelist of the day and the first President of the Anti-Suffrage League, maintained in 1889 that certain government departments should be the exclusive preserve of men:

1   To men belong the struggle of debate and legislation in Parliament; the hard and exhausting labour implied in the administration of the national resources and powers; the conduct of England's relations towards the external world; the working of the army and navy; all the heavy, labori-
5   ous, fundamental industries of the State, such as those of mines, metals, and railways; the lead and supervision of English commerce, the management of our vast English finance, the service of that merchant fleet on which our food supply depends. In all these spheres women's direct participation is made impossible either by the disabilities of sex, or by
10   strong formations of custom and habit resting ultimately upon physical difference, against which it is useless to contend ... Therefore it is not just to give to women direct power of deciding questions of Parliamentary policy, of war, of foreign or colonial affairs, of commerce and finance equal to that possessed by men.[8]

In contrast, women's role was firmly located within the private sphere of the home. Mrs Parker Smith, married to an MP and President of a Scottish Women's Liberal Unionist Association, did not agree with votes for women: she believed that women could never play a full part in public life because of their role as wives and mothers. Family life would be destroyed if women gained the vote, she believed, because women would set about challenging the authority of the male. And as the family was perceived to be the bedrock of society, it followed that society would be destroyed.

The Antis often spoke of politics being too dirty a game for women. Polling booths were considered unfit places for women because men were often bribed with drink, making polling a raucous and disorderly event. Certainly, before the introduction of the secret ballot in 1872, elections were often the excuse for a riotous party. Women were considered far too delicate to enter the fray of this particular form of politics. Antis even argued that sensible men sent their wives and families away from home during elections because they feared for their safety. To involve women in the tumult of politics would be unseemly and to solicit their votes distinctly improper – the very process could defile their natural modesty. As the Liberal Prime Minister Gladstone stated, it would 'trespass upon their delicacy, their purity, their refinement and the elevation of their whole nature'. Not surprisingly it was argued that the courtesies that women received from men would cease if women gained the vote since having the vote would rob them of their feminine charms.

Some Antis certainly viewed the campaign for women's suffrage as the brainchild of a few crazy, dissatisfied spinsters. They drew attention to the small numbers of women who either belonged to suffrage societies or engaged in suffrage activities. They were firmly convinced that the majority of women did not want the vote and were by nature devoid of any direct interest in the affairs of state. Most women, they understood, wished to remain at home looking after their husbands and children and that 'the House of Commons had no right to force upon women a privilege which only a very limited number of their sex asked for'.[9]

c) Male Influence

Antis argued that it was unnecessary for women to be enfranchised because they were already indirectly represented by the men in their family. In the first part of the nineteenth century, they claimed, Parliament represented communities rather than individuals, so a landowner represented the village community, a mine owner the mining community – and a husband the interests of his wife and children. 'Women', said one MP in 1870, 'should be satisfied with the great power they now possess indirectly'. In addition, some women exerted a subtle and indirect control on national affairs as the wives and mothers of powerful men by acting as political hostesses and by seeking conversation with the famous. Both Disraeli and Gladstone, for example, discussed Government secrets with their wives and Winston Churchill was no doubt receptive to the ideas of the distinguished political hostess, Lady Jeune.

Rather inconsistently, fears were also expressed that women were incapable of forming their own opinions and were overly influenced by the men in their lives. Husbands and fathers, in particular, expected their wives and daughters to agree with their political views: opponents suggested that this would have the effect of giving two or more votes to men with close female relatives. In addition, it was feared that religious rivalry, particularly in Ireland, would increase once women were granted the vote. Roman Catholic priests were said to favour female suffrage because of the undue influence they might exercise in the pulpit and the confessional. This would have the effect of increasing the Catholic vote, which in turn might create further tensions between Catholic and non-Catholic communities as the former demanded greater equality.

Antis actually went so far as to believe that the moral and social order would collapse if women were enfranchised: they would not listen to men. On the assumption that electors voted according to their own self-interest, women were expected to vote for issues relevant to their own gender roles. Antis argued that women would vote as women rather than as individuals and would seek to legislate for social reform and against male interests. For example, great concern was expressed that women might vote for temperance reform and ban the sale of alcohol. And as women would predominate in an electorate (in 1929, when women voted in the first universal suffrage election, they constituted 52.7 per cent of the electorate) they would conceivably succeed.

d) Women's Influence Outside Parliament

By the beginning of the twentieth century, however, not all Antis considered that women were basically inferior. A number of Antis distinguished between local government (with its focus on social welfare) and national government (with its focus on international and diplomatic affairs). Mrs Humphrey Ward, for example, thought it appropriate for women to engage in local politics: it was housekeeping on a grander scale and so did not undermine the principles of the separate spheres. She argued that women should elevate the tone of public office through their religious, educational and charitable work rather than busy themselves with national politics. The following leaflet, while recognising that women played an important part in local government, argued that Parliament should remain the province of men:

Against Woman Suffrage by Grace Saxon Mills
(early twentieth century)

1   **Because** women already have the municipal vote, and are eligible for membership of most local authorities. These bodies deal with questions of housing, education, care of children, workhouses and so forth, all of which are peculiarly within a woman's sphere.

5   Parliament, however, has to deal mainly with the administration of a vast Empire, the maintenance of the Army and Navy, and with questions of peace and war, which lie outside the legitimate sphere of woman's influence.

Because all government rests ultimately on force, to which
10   women, owing to physical, moral and social reasons, are not capable of contributing.

Because women are not capable of full citizenship, for the simple reason that they are not available for purposes of national and Imperial defence. All government rests ultimately on force, to
15   which women, owing to physical, moral and social reasons, are not capable of contributing.

Because there is little doubt that the vast majority of women have no desire for the vote.

Because the acquirement of the Parliamentary vote would logi-
20   cally involve admission to Parliament itself, and to all Government offices. It is scarcely possible to imagine a woman being Minister for War, and yet the principles of the Suffragettes involve that and many similar absurdities.

Because the United Kingdom is not an isolated state, but the
25   administrative and governing centre of a system of colonies and also of dependencies. The effect of introducing a large female element into the Imperial electorate would undoubtedly be to weaken the centre of power in the eyes of these dependent millions.

30   **Because** past legislation in Parliament shows that the interests of women are perfectly safe in the hands of men.

Because Woman Suffrage is based on the idea of the equality of the sexes, and tends to establish those competitive relations which will destroy chivalrous consideration.

35   **Because** women have at present a vast indirect influence through their menfolk on the politics of this country.

Because the physical nature of women unfits them for direct competition with men.

3 Conclusion

> **KEY ISSUE** Which side would you take in the debate over
> women's suffrage?

Both sides advanced powerful arguments, but it is fair to say that, at
first, the Antis seemed to be winning. The campaign for votes for
women was treated as a joke by large numbers of people in Britain.
Early suffragists had to be particularly careful in their speeches and
their leaflets to advance a rational defence, whereas all the Antis had
to do to gain support was to laugh at them. By 1914, however, many
of the ideas of the Antis appeared ludicrously old-fashioned and it was
evident that the argument in favour of votes for women had, more or
less, been won. Both sides, however, considered that their own particular assertions were correct and, therefore, the debate could not be
decided intellectually. Instead, political pressure would play a decisive
role in the case for and against women's suffrage.

Suffragists and suffragettes developed numerous justifications for
women's franchise but what is remarkable is the consistency of those
arguments over time. Indeed there were no specifically 'suffragist' and
'suffragette' justifications. Both groups claimed the right for women
to vote on the same terms as men in Parliamentary elections. However, as the nineteenth century progressed, the meaning of this
demand changed. If the first women's suffrage bill had been passed
in 1870 it would have been decidedly elitist, as only a very few rich
women would have been enfranchised. By 1914, when the property
qualifications for men was much lower, more and more women would
have been eligible to vote if the terms had been the same. What did
change was the confidence with which the case was argued: whereas
early suffragists argued their points very tentatively, the Edwardian
suffragettes, more secure in the justice of their cause, produced the
most startling propaganda. Similarly, both the suffragists and the suffragettes saw the vote as a symbol of citizenship in a democratic country
and made the case that women had the right to be represented.

It used to be assumed that whereas the suffragists wanted the vote
as a means to an end, the suffragettes wanted the vote as an end in itself,
but this interpretation has recently been revised. The literature produced by both groups suggests that they wanted the vote to end the
economic, social and moral exploitation of women. However, there
were some differences in practice. For example, Victorian suffragists
were more reluctant to associate sexual morality with the vote because
they felt this would do harm to the suffrage cause. In contrast, the
Edwardians had few such qualms: Christabel Pankhurst, for instance,
promoted votes for women and chastity for men simultaneously.

The arguments of the Antis, on the other hand, grew more rational
over time. When the idea of women's suffrage was first debated, it was

considered so ridiculous that the Antis did not bother to marshal any sensible argument against it at all. This changed by the end of the nineteenth century as a better organised women's suffrage movement emerged and the Antis were put on the defensive. Nevertheless, there were different shades of opinion: Mrs Humphrey Ward, for example, maintained that women were different from but not unequal to men while others continued to stress women's innate inferiority.

Although the arguments used by those who supported and those who opposed women's suffrage differed in significant ways, there were some surprising similarities. Firstly, both sides had no desire to undermine women's domestic role. Those who supported female suffrage believed that women's unique capabilities would improve government; but the Antis who shared the conviction that women's talents originated in the home, believed that they should remain there. Secondly, most of those involved in the suffrage debate seemed to believe that votes for women was the means to an end. The suffragists, suffragettes and the Antis all held that the vote would bring about a social revolution, but whereas the former welcomed such change it struck fear into the opposition. Suffragists and suffragettes looked forward to the day when women would be able to end the perceived exploitation of their sex by instituting changes to the law and increasing educational and employment opportunities for women. For them, the vote would herald a new dawn of equality. In contrast, the Antis feared the reforming zeal of enfranchised women because it would undermine the authority of the male. One late nineteenth-century MP maintained that a Parliament elected by women would 'have more class cries, permissive legislation, domestic perplexities, and sentimental grievances' and give greater importance to questions of a social nature, at the expense of constitutional and international issues.

Thirdly, the suffragists, the suffragettes and their opponents recognised women's contribution to local government. Those who supported women's suffrage used this to convince people of women's ability to engage in national politics, whereas the Antis used the same argument to demonstrate that women had already fulfiled their political potential. In fact, some Antis considered local government to be women's proper sphere because it concerned education, health and housing. Finally, both the Suffragists and the Antis were conscious of Britain's role as an imperial power and used this to argue either for or against votes for women. At times both used white supremacist arguments: the suffragists believing that white women should gain the vote before black men; the Antis believing that black men would not accept the authority of women whatever their colour. Such similarities are perhaps not surprising, as after all the suffragists, the suffragettes and their opponents inhabited the same cultural world and historical period. And of course one has to have common areas of agreement in order to disagree!

By the beginning of the twentieth century votes for women had become difficult to refute. The arguments put forward by the Antis lost their force. Suffrage campaigners may have won the debate but those who opposed them drew on the fact that most women remained indifferent to the franchise, some were opposed and very few campaigned for it. Certainly, although most MPs now favoured women's suffrage, Government still had to be convinced that the cause was genuinely popular. As one MP put it, the Government 'could not consent to make a revolution for a handful of fanatics'. Hence suffrage action began to speak louder than words.

References

1 *Representative Government,* John Stuart Mill (OUP, 1960 reprint) p. 22.
2 'The Great Scourge and How to Fight It', by Christabel Pankhurst in *The Sexuality Debates,* S. Jeffreys (Routledge and Kegan Paul, 1987), p. 318.
3 'The White Woman's Burden, British Feminists and the Indian Woman, 1865–1915' by Antoinette Burton in *Women's Studies International Forum,* 1990, p. 295.
4 Quoted in *Feminism and Democracy,* Sandra Holton (Cambridge University Press, 1986) p. 4.
5 *Fate Has Been Kind,* Frederick Pethick Lawrence (Hutchinson, 1943) p. 68.
6 Asquith, in *Separate Spheres: The Opposition to Women's Suffrage in Britain,* Brian Harrison (Croom Helm, 1978), p. 33.
7 Mrs Frederick Harrison, 1909, ibid, p. 80.
8 From *Before the Vote was Won,* Jane Lewis (Routledge and Kegan Paul, 1987), p. 409.
9 Ibid, p. 65.

Summary Diagram

Votes for women: the debate

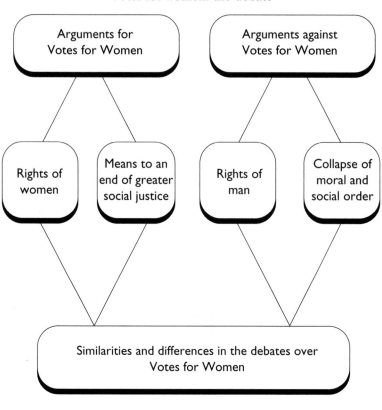

Working on Chapter 2

This chapter outlines the main debates about why women should or should not have the vote. It is important that you understand the development of women's demands and how they emerged alongside the struggles for Parliamentary Reform in the years 1832–80. At the same time you need to be aware of the changing economic, social and political positions of women within society. After reading this chapter you should realise that women wanted the vote for a number of reasons. Using the sub-headings as a guide construct a checklist of the arguments for and against why the vote should be granted to women. Consider who opposed the extension of the franchise in this period and the significance of this.

Answering essay questions on Chapter 2

Many of the questions on the topic covered in this chapter will revolve around how and why the suffragists and suffragettes struggled to get their message across to those who opposed the right of women to have the vote.

Consider the following questions:

a) To what extent did the arguments of those who opposed and those who supported women's suffrage in the years 1880–1914 differ?

Examiners will be looking for a clear exposition on the two positions of those who opposed and those who supported the political rights of women. You need to consider why there was so much opposition to women having the vote and the implications of this for opposition to the NUWSS and the WSPU.

b) To what extent was the changing role of women in the years 1860–1914 due to wider changes in society rather than the actions of individuals?

Answering source-based questions on Chapter 2

1 Pro- and Anti-Suffrage views
   Read the extracts by Mrs Ward (page 23) and from the leaflet written by the NUWSS (page 20) and answer the following questions:

   a) What can you learn from Mrs Ward about the attitudes of those opposed to votes for women? (*10 marks*)
   b) In what ways do the attitudes expressed in the leaflet refute those of the opposition? (*10 marks*)
   c) Using these sources and your own knowledge, explain the similarities and differences between those who supported and those who opposed votes for women. (*25 marks*)

3 Suffragists and Suffragettes

The two most well-known women's suffrage groups are the National Union of Women's Suffrage Societies (NUWSS), known as the suffragists, and the Women's Social and Political Union (WSPU), known as the suffragettes. This chapter will show that the women's suffrage movement was more diverse than these groups suggest. It will go on to argue that the women's suffrage movement of both the nineteenth and twentieth centuries was characterised by arguments over policy. There were frequent divisions and splits. You may like to consider the reasons for these splits, whether they could have been avoided and the extent to which the disagreements helped women find the best political way forward for votes for women. You may also like to decide whether or not you think the WSPU was an autocratic organisation. If you had lived in this period, to which group would you have belonged?

KEY DATES

1832 First suffrage petition to Parliament
1847 First leaflet on female suffrage published
1851 Sheffield Association for Female Franchise
1865 Committee for Women's Suffrage
1866 Women's Suffrage Provisional Committee
1867 First permanent women's suffrage society in Manchester
1868 National Society for Women's Suffrage (NSWS)
1870 Women's Suffrage Journal
1871 London National Society for Women's Suffrage (LNSWS)
1872 Central Committee of National Society for Women's Suffrage (CCNS)
1877 New Central Committee of National Society for Women's Suffrage united LNSWS and CCNS
1888 Central National Committee of Women's Suffrage. Central Committee of National Society for Women's Suffrage
1890 Women's Franchise League
1892 Women's Emancipation League
1897 National Union of Women's Suffrage Societies (NUWSS)
1903 Women's Social and Political Union Lancashire and Cheshire Women Textile and Other Workers Representative Committee (LCWT)
1907 Women's Freedom League

1 The Origins of Women's Suffrage

> **KEY ISSUE** Why did women in the women's suffrage movement disagree with each other so much?

a) Introduction

In 1860, when this book begins, there were no women's suffrage societies campaigning for votes for women whatsoever, but by 1914 there were approximately 56 groups with a combined membership of 300,000. It is difficult to trace the origins of the women's suffrage movement that operated in late Victorian and Edwardian Britain since, like most political crusades, it had somewhat confused and erratic beginnings. The suffrage movement began slowly with several people in different towns thinking and agitating around similar issues, in this case the vote. Some historians date the movement from 1832, when Mary Smith presented the first women's suffrage petition to Parliament. The letters and the leaflets distributed in support of women's suffrage by Anne Knight in 1847, and the Sheffield Female Political Association formed in 1851, are also considered key moments of suffrage history.[1] Others date the origins of the suffrage movement much later and suggest that it really took off in 1867, when John Stuart Mill moved an amendment to the Second Reform Bill asking that the word 'man' be replaced by 'person'. Even before a movement emerged the publication of certain texts – Mary Wollstonecraft's *A Vindication of the Rights of Women* in 1792; William Thompson's wordily titled *Appeal of One Half of the Human Race, Women, Against the Pretensions of the Other Half, Men, to Retain Them in Political, and Thence in Civil and Domestic, Slavery* in 1825; and Harriet Taylor and J S Mill's *The Subjection of Women* in 1869 – established the intellectual argument for votes for women.

Historians nevertheless agree that London and Manchester were the major suffragist centres and that the year 1866 was a significant landmark in suffragist history. In response to a promise by J S Mill that he would introduce a women's suffrage amendment to Disraeli's 1867 Reform Bill, some of the most notable feminist campaigners of the nineteenth century – Barbara Bodichon, Emily Davies, Jessie Boucherett, Elizabeth Garrett and Helen Taylor – drafted a petition to Parliament demanding the enfranchisement of all householders regardless of sex. Emily Davies and Elizabeth Garrett carried the petition, signed by almost 1500 women, to the House of Commons where two of the handful of sympathetic MPs, J S Mill and Henry Fawcett, presented it. In 1866 too, the Manchester National Society for Women's Suffrage was formed by Lydia Becker, followed shortly after by similar organisations in Birmingham, Bristol, Edinburgh and Ireland. Each of these groups was independent but it soon became obvious that there would be benefits in having a federal union. In

1868, encouraged by Lydia Becker, all of these regional societies amalgamated to become the National Society for Women's Suffrage. This, according to most historians, was the moment when organised national action began.

b) Uneasy Alliances

This unity was not to last. The early women's suffrage movement was characterised by internal factions as the suffragists, and later the suffragettes, differed over the best way to achieve their objective. Consequently, those campaigning for votes for women have had a rather complex and chequered history, which the summary below helps to explain.

At the outset, the London suffrage group witnessed a number of disagreements over strategy between two of the most powerful advocates of women's suffrage: Helen Taylor and Barbara Bodichon. Helen Taylor wanted a woman-only Committee whereas Barbara Bodichon believed that men should also be involved. These internal wranglings led to many suffragists disassociating themselves from the London group, thus weakening the emerging women's movement. It is not surprising therefore that the first London society was thought by many to be ineffective.

In 1871 another split occurred between London and the rest of the country in response to the Ladies' National Association's (LNA) campaigns against the Contagious Diseases Acts (CDAs) (see page 6). On the one hand members of the provincial suffrage societies considered the LNA and the women's suffrage movement to be part of the same struggle against female oppression. In their opinion, the CDAs were part of a male conspiracy by a male Parliament and would not have been passed if women had voting power. On the other hand, the London National Society for Women's Suffrage wished to keep women's suffrage distinct from other political protest groups, not because they were antagonistic to the LNA, but because they feared it might create unnecessary enemies for the suffrage cause. As a consequence, the NSWS split into two, and not until 1877 did the two organisations reunite to form the Central Committee of the National Society, with Lydia Becker later becoming Secretary.

At the end of 1888 yet another split occurred, precipitated by two major disagreements over political strategy. Firstly a number of the younger and more radical suffragists wanted to affiliate to the women's section of the Liberal Association because the Liberal Party was perceived to be sympathetic to votes for women. Others – mostly the older members – disagreed because they wanted to keep the suffrage organisation independent of party politics. Secondly, younger members wanted to link suffrage with other female reforms (in particular the campaign for greater property rights), while the older members preferred to keep suffrage distinct. Once again the suffrage movement split into two, rather confusingly named, groups: the Central National Society for Women's Suffrage and the Central Committee of the National Society for Women's Suffrage led by Millicent Fawcett. Lydia Becker, who had devoted her entire life to the suffrage movement, regarded the Central National Society to which Emmeline and her husband Richard Pankhurst belonged, as left-wing and extreme.

Soon members were disagreeing with the policies of the newly formed Central National Society (CNS). The CNS wanted to restrict the vote to single women, which meant that married women would be excluded from the franchise. This policy was criticised because it sacrificed the rights of married women to achieve a limited goal. 'I think,' Richard Pankhurst argued, 'it would push back freedom for married women certainly twenty or five-and-twenty years'.[2] The question of which women should be given the vote was a matter of deep contention within the suffrage movement. Some suffragists insisted that it was better to have a small reform rather than no reform at all and so the Women's Franchise League (WFrL) was established. From the very beginning, this new organisation, like the CNS before it, identified with the Liberal Party. It was also the first women's suffrage society to include married women in the franchise. The WFrL had two main aims, firstly 'to extend to women, whether unmarried, married or widowed, the right to vote at Parliamentary, Municipal, Local and other elections' on the same terms as men, and secondly to 'establish for all women equal civil and political rights with men'.[3]

The WFrL was a small organisation. In early 1890, according to Elizabeth Crawford, it had 140 members and £70 in the bank. Even though it was small the WFrL was influential. It included many of the leading political activists of the period: Jacob Bright (radical MP), Josephine Butler (leader of the campaign to abolish the Contagious Diseases Acts), Elizabeth Wolstenholme Elmy (a radical suffragist), William Lloyd Garrison (a former slave and American activist) and Harriot Stanton Blatch (an American suffragist). The WFrL attracted top Liberal support. In November 1889, they hosted a well-attended meeting at which R B Haldane (Liberal MP) was a keynote speaker.

The WFrL made a number of attempts to bridge the suffrage gap and to re-unite the suffrage movement but the other societies were reluctant to join. A leading member of the NSWS, Mrs Eva McLaren, 'said that as Dr. Pankhurst showed signs of his intention to boss the whole business, they [i.e. the NSWS] had backed out and declined further union'.[4] Moreover, even this small group could not agree on policy and a year later another split occurred. In April 1892 the Pankhursts led a disturbance at a suffrage meeting organised by Lydia Becker in St James' Hall. At the time a Parliamentary Franchise Bill, put forward as a private member's bill by the Conservative MP Albert Rollit, was being discussed in Parliament. Lydia Becker, who called the meeting in support of Rollitt, championed this Bill, which would enfranchise single but not married women. Both Pankhursts heckled the speakers: they interrupted proceedings by shouting their objections to this limited franchise and demanding that married women be included. The effect of the Pankhursts' behaviour was to produce further splits within the suffrage movement. Elizabeth Wolstenholme Elmy, critical of their disorderly behaviour, resigned from her position as Secretary of the Women's Franchise League and set up the Women's Emancipation Union.

When Elmy resigned, Ursula Bright, a friend and colleague of Emmeline Pankhurst, was promoted to the post of Secretary. Pankhurst and Bright – supported by their sympathetic husbands – worked hard to promote female equality and their efforts finally bore fruit in the 1894 Local Government Act. This Act enshrined the principle that all women, whether married or single, should be entitled to vote in local elections if they possessed the necessary property qualifications. Ursula Bright's husband, Jacob, was primarily responsible for securing this municipal franchise while Richard Pankhurst had drafted the Bill. Not surprisingly, Emmeline and Ursula were delighted. In a triumphalist letter to her friend, Ursula commented that the other two, rival, societies 'are simply mad at our success. They never calculated upon such a decisive victory ... it will be impossible to carry a Parliamentary spinster's Bill if the married women are locally enfranchised'.[5] In fact, the assertion that it would now be impossible to exclude married women from the franchise was prophetic: the 1894 Local Government Act had the effect of collapsing many of the old animosities between different suffrage societies. With married women safely enfranchised in local government it seemed nonsensical, and possibly even churlish, to insist that only single women be given the vote. By the end of the nineteenth century, all suffrage societies were committed to campaign for women to be given the vote on the same terms as men.

It is important to remember that the continuous bickering and disagreements within the suffrage movement were good for the refinement of ideas and policy. Indeed the splits and divisions that occurred within Societies can be seen to have had a positively creative and generative function – their dynamics were instrumental in shaping new organisational directions for the twentieth century.[6] More importantly for Emmeline Pankhurst's own political career, she learned a very great deal about strategic planning even though the WFrL itself was very short-lived. As Harriet Stanton Blatch later wrote of the WFrL, 'there rose from its ashes the militant work of the WSPU in England and the work of the Women's Political Union in America'.[7]

2 The NUWSS and its Offshoots: 1897–1914

KEY ISSUE How did the NUWSS keep the suffrage movement united?

Eventually in 1897 most of the various suffrage societies united once more under the federal structure of the National Union of Women's Suffrage Societies (NUWSS). At first the NUWSS co-ordinated the work of the local suffrage societies and liaised between them and MPs in the House of Commons. This loose federation meant that local groups could develop independent policies without alienating others and splitting the organisation. Unity was therefore achieved but at a cost. The NUWSS had no real authority over the various groups, no funds of its own to promote women's suffrage and no autonomous Executive Committee.

Throughout this period there was a high level of social homogeneity (that is uniformity) within the suffrage movement since most of the leaders shared a family and friendship circle and held similar political convictions and religious beliefs. Although the NUWSS claimed to be non-party political, many suffragists had links with the Liberal Party or were sympathetic to Liberal aims and had access to the Liberal political elite. Many were also joint members of the Women's Liberal Federation and the NUWSS and were often the wives, mothers or daughters of prominent Liberal politicians. For example, Helen Taylor, the daughter of Harriet Taylor, enjoyed an unusually close relationship with her step-father, the highly respected Liberal philosopher John Stuart Mill, who championed the cause of women's suffrage in Parliament. Similarly, Catherine Osler, leader of the Birmingham NUWSS and President of the Women's Auxiliary of the Liberal Association, was sister-in-law to the prominent Liberal Joseph Chamberlain. Indeed, there were 'suffrage families' such as Priscilla Bright MacLaren's: her brother, the Liberal MP Jacob Bright, had defended women's suffrage in Parliament and her sons and daughters-in-law were all women's suffrage activists. Of course, not all suffragists were Liberal sympathisers: France Power Cobbe (feminist and anti-vivisectionist) and Emily Davies (educational campaigner) were staunch Conservatives.

Politics was firmly linked to religion. A number of suffragists came from Nonconformist radical backgrounds in which political and social reform was on the agenda: apparently 20 per cent of the executive of the NUWSS were Quakers. It is not surprising that, given their political and religious background, many suffragist leaders belonged to families who were committed to social reform in a wider context. The Quaker suffragist Anne Knight was actively involved in the abolitionist movement, supported free trade, the Chartists and sympathised with European republicanism. Lydia Becker, the first national secretary of the NSWS, was active in various campaigns such as the campaign against the CDAs and reform of married women's property. In 1870 she founded the first women's suffrage journal, which she edited until her death 20 years later. Her successor, Millicent Fawcett, was the daughter of a merchant who was sympathetic to feminism, the younger sister of the first English female doctor, the widow of a former Liberal Cabinet Minister, and a close friend of John Stuart Mill (see biography for further details).

Not surprisingly, many suffragists were involved in other women's rights issues. Both Barbara Bodichon and Emmeline Wolstoneholme Elmy had led campaigns to reform the Married Women's Property Acts (see page 5). Experience such as this provided a bridge between women's traditional role in the private sphere of the home and their future one in the public sphere of political struggle. And of course the kinship, friendship, religious and political circle to which they belonged provided women with the emotional and moral support needed to lead an unconventional campaign.

The examples of suffrage personnel given above show that the early suffrage movement was predominantly a middle-class movement. However, in their thought-provoking book *One Hand Tied Behind Us*, Liddington and Norris break the myth that the suffrage movement was completely dominated by the middle class. Certainly, the membership of the NUWSS was socially mixed in the north of England. In some areas like Oldham it was predominantly middle-class, whereas a few miles away in Clitheroe the membership was exclusively working-class. One of the associations affiliated to the NUWSS, the North of England Society for Women's Suffrage, was committed to broadening the class composition of the suffrage movement and so put a great deal of effort into recruiting working-class women.

Nevertheless, there were certain tensions between the older middle-class members of the NUWSS and the newer working-class recruits of the North of England Society. In 1903 the Lancashire and Cheshire Women Textile and Other Workers' Representation Committee (LCWT) was founded specifically for working-class women. Although it was set up by the university educated Esther Roper and the aristocratic Eva Gore-Booth, they encouraged working-class women to participate at a senior level: several textile workers and trade union activists took a leading role in the North of England Society. Not surprisingly, the LCWT worked closely with the Women's Co-operative Guild and the Manchester and Salford Women's Trade Union Council, of which Eva Gore-Booth was Co-Secretary. Although the LCWT had broken away from the NUWSS, the two groups – unlike those of the nineteenth century – were not antagonistic towards each other. On the contrary, the LCWT received a lot of financial help from the NUWSS with the result that it was able to establish support for women's suffrage in the textile towns of the north of England.

By the end of the nineteenth century the women's suffrage movement appeared to be united and strong. In 1907 the NUWSS adopted a new constitution that gave its executive the power to make decisions, hire its own staff and to control financial spending. It also elected Millicent Fawcett as its first President. By 1909 NUWSS employed ten organisers, had published its first newspaper, The Common Cause, and had 207 groups affiliated to it. This unprecedented growth led to further re-structuring. The NUWSS divided its regional groups into independent federations headed by their own committees. Just before the outbreak of war there were approximately 600 such groups in England, Scotland and Wales, all affiliated to the NUWSS. However, the suffragists were to face new challenges in the early twentieth century when a new organisation, the Women's Social and Political Union (WSPU) erupted onto the political scene.

MILLICENT GARRETT FAWCETT 1847–1929   *- Profile -*

Millicent Garrett Fawcett, the daughter of Newson Garrett and Louise Dunnell was born at Aldeburgh, a small, sleepy fishing village on the Suffolk coast. Millicent gained her political education from her family. In July 1865 she was taken by two of her sisters to listen to an election speech by J S Mill who in turn introduced her to other radicals like Henry Fawcett, a blind Liberal MP, whom she later married. In 1867, a year after their marriage, their only child, Philippa, was born. At first, Millicent concentrated on helping her husband with his constituency work but gradually she became involved in women's rights and began writing articles and books.

In 1868 Millicent joined the London Suffrage Committee and spoke at many meetings in support of votes for women. She joined the Central Committee for Women's Suffrage (CCWS) in 1874, joined the executive of the New Central Committee of the National Society for Women's Suffrage (NSWS) in 1877 when the suffrage movement once more re-united. She became a Liberal Unionist in 1886; and not wishing the NSWS to be affiliated to the Liberal Party, she took the side of the Central National Committee of Women's Suffrage when the movement once again split into two.

Millicent Fawcett was not a naturally gifted speaker but she quickly established a reputation as an exceptional organiser and emerged as the natural leader of the NUWSS when it was established. In 1907 she became its first President. In 1912, wearied by Liberal unwillingness to grant votes to women, she, and the NUWSS, turned to the Labour Party for support.

As with other suffragists, Millicent Fawcett was involved in other campaigns to promote equality for women in education, work and the law. She also supported the work of Josephine Butler and was active in the campaigns against the white slave traffic. In honour of her contributions she was elected President of the National Council of Women.

3 The WSPU and its Offshoots: 1903–14

> **KEY ISSUES** Why was the WSPU run on such autocratic lines? To
> what extent did it abandon its working-class roots?

a) Structure of the Organisation

In 1903 Emmeline Pankhurst, who had been active in previous suffrage campaigns, founded the Women's Social and Political Union
(WSPU) at her house in Manchester. The women present at the meeting wanted to cast off the Liberal image of women's suffrage, to reverse
the decades of sufffrage defeat and turn the WSPU into a viable political machine that achieved results. In her autobiography Emmeline
Pankhurst stated that she wanted to keep the WSPU free from party
affiliation, yet at first the WSPU was very sympathetic to the Labour
Party and its early membership consisted of Labour Party activists.

The WSPU has been accused of being an autocratic, man-hating,
organisation that was considerably less democratic than its rival. From
1906, policies were decided by an unelected Central Committee with
Sylvia Pankhurst as secretary, Emmeline Pethick-Lawrence as Treasurer
and Annie Kenney as paid organiser. This Central Committee was
assisted by a sub-committee that consisted mainly of family and friends
of the Pankhursts. Mary Clarke (Emmeline Pankhurst's sister), for
example, served on this sub-committee. Members did not participate
in decision-making but were informed of new policies and strategies
during the 'At Homes' sessions, which were held each Monday after-
noon at the headquarters in Lincoln's Inn Field, London. The leadership controlled all publications, all appointments to paid positions
and of course the organisation's finances. It was difficult, if not
impossible, for members to oppose them.

Many have criticised this structure. Ray Strachey, for instance, suggests that the WSPU 'entrusted all their decisions to their leaders …
These people alone decided what was to be done; the others obeyed,
and enjoyed the surrender of their judgement, and the sensation of
marching as an army under discipline'.[8] David Mitchell not only enti-
tles the last chapter of his book, *Queen Christabel*, 'Bitch Power', as
an unflattering description of the suffragettes and their successors,
but compares the WSPU with a German terrorist gang.[9] Socialist
feminist historians, although using different terminology, subscribe
to this interpretation: Liddington and Norris believe that the leadership
of the WSPU exercised draconian control over its membership.
One suffragette at the time commented that although Emmeline
Pankhurst 'wishes women to have votes she will not allow them to have
opinions'.[10]

The WSPU's unitary command structure, its family cabal of leaders
and its dismissal of debate seem to be strangely at odds with its

demands for democracy. Critics disapproved of the organisational structure of the WSPU for a number of reasons: it was considered hypocritical of the WSPU to condemn the Liberal Government for its reluctance to widen the suffrage while failing to practise democracy itself. Democracy is usually based on discussion, freedom of expression, constitutional procedures and consensus and these the WSPU leaders certainly did not practise. It was also believed that the vote should be sought through a democratic organisation that mirrored a future body politic rather than one that clearly did not; and it was thought that unquestioning obedience to a female oligarchy was inadequate preparation for the future female voter, who needed to evaluate the arguments of each political party. Moreover, the WSPU's espousal of a militant strategy seems to hold the principles of democratic process in contempt.

However, although the WSPU was undoubtedly dictatorial in style and had no formal constitution, there are a number of points to take into consideration before it is condemned out of hand. Firstly, critics of the WSPU's structure are largely those in sympathy with the NUWSS and who thus take sides in the suffrage struggle. Secondly, the WSPU was not always undemocratic. Initially it favoured an informal approach to politics – there was no official membership list and any woman who wished to attend a meeting was welcome. In the beginning neither Christabel nor Emmeline Pankhurst took an officer role because they feared their new organisation might be dubbed the Pankhurst family party. As time went on, it is true, the WSPU did become more formalised and less democratic. Nevertheless, nobody was forced to belong to the organisation and members could always leave if they disagreed with the policies. Moreover, the suffragettes of the WSPU were not meek and mild individuals with no will of their own: these women were strong political activists who would not listen to or obey those with whom they disagreed or disapproved.

Thirdly, as both Emmeline and Christabel Pankhurst argued, a democratic organisation was probably inappropriate for their style of politics. Indeed the WSPU became less democratic as its activities became more illegal. And as the WSPU increasingly operated within a hostile political climate, so military-style planning, command and action assumed greater importance than constitutional democracy. Certainly, Emmeline and Christabel Pankhurst's charismatic style of leadership meant they could make up policy on the hoof rather than wait for endless committees to debate and agree new decisions. Emmeline in particular was highly intuitive. She relied more on her inner feelings, on her natural empathy, than on her intellectual powers. She instinctively 'knew' how to respond to the quickening pace of events and grass-roots members who inaugurated new policy initiatives soon had them adopted and developed by their leader. Rank and file members certainly adored the WSPU leader: Emmeline maintained her position by sheer force of personality rather than by election, by charm rather than by fear. Wherever she and Christabel went and wherever they spoke, suffragette audiences gave them standing ovations, preferring to relinquish democracy rather than lose their beloved leaders.

Fourthly, the WSPU did educate its membership, encouraged their self-confidence and helped to develop political awareness. Many suffragettes told how they were taught the skills of public speaking and debate. Finally, although the London-based WSPU was undoubtedly undemocratic, this may not have been the case for the provincial branches and their regional offices. In 1909 there were at least 11 regional offices, in the West of England (with offices in Bristol and Torquay), Lancashire (with offices in Manchester, Preston and Rochdale), Birmingham, Leeds, Newcastle, Glasgow, Edinburgh and Aberdeen. For the most part, these branches and offices enjoyed considerable autonomy, as the following extract from an Annual Report suggests:

1 In all parts of London and in many provincial centres, there exist local
    Unions which, while working in close and harmonious relation with the
    National headquarters, are independent in the sense that they elect
    their own committee, and administer their own funds ... and arrange
5 their own schemes of organisation and propaganda.[11]

The East London Federation of Suffragettes (ELFS), a working-class branch of the WSPU organised by Sylvia, another daughter of Emmeline Pankhurst, was certainly run on democratic lines. Here officers and delegates stood for election and were voted in. The points outlined above may not overthrow the hostile criticism made of the WSPU but they certainly modify it by explaining the context in which the suffragettes worked.

Concern is also expressed by historians that the suffragettes were anti-male. It is certainly true that the WSPU would not allow men to join the organisation and continually affirmed women's independence from the opposite sex. Yet the WSPU initially welcomed male support. In particular, it appreciated the advice of Frederick Pethick-Lawrence who helped edit Votes for Women and whose business acumen helped lift the economic fortunes of the WSPU from a small provincial society to a great business enterprise. Nonetheless, by 1913 the WSPU was unwilling to co-operate with men or with other organisations, like the NUWSS, which had male associates. Radical feminist historians are not so critical of this shift for they view the WSPU as the first autonomous women's organisation and therefore the precursor of the women's liberation movement of the late 1960s.

b) Suffragette Membership

One of the major criticisms levelled against the WSPU relates to its membership, which is compared unfavourably with that of the

NUWSS. Historians have argued that the WSPU was an elitist organisation committed to an elitist franchise. Certainly, the WSPU was associated with middle-class and aristocratic spinsters who wanted a limited franchise based on property qualifications rather than universal suffrage. However, this criticism needs to be reassessed. The founder of the WSPU, Emmeline Pankhurst, came from a similar social background to the members of the NUWSS. She, like Millicent Fawcett, came from a long line of male political activists: granddaughter of a man who had demonstrated at Peterloo, daughter of a radical cotton manufacturer, and wife of Richard Pankhurst, a left-wing lawyer. What is more, the WSPU at first recruited greater numbers of working-class women than the NUWSS, for the roots of the WSPU lay in the Labour politics of the north of England rather than the Liberal salons of the south. The WSPU was set up specifically for working-class women and between 1903 and 1906 its members did valuable propaganda work in the textile towns. Even when the WSPU's headquarters moved to London it targeted working-class women. When Annie Kenney, a cotton worker recruited at a WSPU meeting in Oldham, was sent to London with Sylvia Pankhurst to organise the campaign in the capital most of their energies were spent in working-class districts. Moreover, the first London branch of the WSPU was formed at Canning Town in the East End.

Yet, when Christabel Pankhurst arrived in London working-class women receded into the background of the WSPU to be replaced by women of an entirely different social class. The most famous example was the aristocratic and politically Conservative Constance Lytton, whose father had been one of the Viceroys of India and whose mother had been lady-in-waiting to Queen Victoria. Historians have condemned the WSPU for recruiting upper-class women. Andrew Rosen, for example, regrets the decline of working-class membership, particularly when the WSPU 'ceased to envisage votes for women as a measure desirable primarily because it would benefit working-class women'.[12] Liddington and Norris, too, criticise the WSPU because it had little sustained contact with working-class women.

In many ways this analysis only really applies to the central London section, for the WSPU's strength lay with its local branches as much as its headquarters. Until 1908 the WSPU was active in Woolwich, Lewisham and Greenwich, working with the local Labour Party to recruit working-class women. In 1913, as Krista Cowman points out, the WSPU remained true to its socialist past by inviting a local ILP leader to open its new offices in Liverpool.[13] Sylvia Pankhurst's ELFS remained a working-class organisation and 'regarded itself as part of the labour movement, for it saw the achievement of equality and emancipation as inseparable from a socialist organisation of society'.[14] In Scotland too the links with working-class women and socialism remained strong. Furthermore, whatever its class composition, the WSPU consistently supported issues relating to working-class women.

For instance, when working-class women such as pit-brow workers, chain-makers and barmaids, had their livelihoods threatened, they all received support from the WSPU.

It could also be argued that the recruitment of middle- and upper-class women to the WSPU may not have been a weakness at all because this broadening of its class composition made it less exclusive. More-over, in bringing women from different classes together, the WSPU helped weaken the class divisions which characterised Edwardian Britain. Certainly the WSPU saw the unity of women as more import-ant than the division of class and suggested that the subordination of women to men was as at least as significant as class oppression. This

Front page of *The Suffragette*, 17 January 1913.

prompted the radical feminist historian Elizabeth Sarah to argue that 'what these early feminists were doing was laying claims to sexual equality by challenging the power of men'.[15] By 1914 Christabel Pankhurst undoubtedly treated all men as enemies, complained that socialist men – despite their commitment to equality – were little better than the Conservatives and Liberals in their failure to support votes for women and even considered her godfather Frederick Pethick-Lawrence (who had devoted his life to the cause) to be an embarrassment purely because he was a man.

c) Divisions within the WSPU

It is sometimes argued that splits in the WSPU arose primarily because the Pankhursts were ruthless in getting rid of those who criticised their personal control. Between 1903 and 1914 there were several splits in the WSPU, of which the three most important occurred in 1907, 1912 and 1914, respectively. The first involved Teresa Billington-Greig, Charlotte Despard and others; the second the Pethick-Lawrences; and the third Sylvia Pankhurst.

During 1907 differences came to a head between Charlotte Despard, Teresa Billington-Greig and Emmeline Pankhurst. The first two complained that the WSPU was turning its back on the working class and cultivating upper-class and wealthy women. More importantly, Teresa Billington-Greig wanted greater organisational democracy and more independence for the branches. In 1906 she drafted a democratic constitution for the WSPU proposing annual conferences with elected leaders and members who could vote. In effect, the proposed constitution, which had been accepted by much of the membership, placed power in the hands of the branch delegates at the expense of the leadership. Unfortunately for Billington-Greig, Emmeline and Christabel Pankhurst disagreed with it, and in a well-orchestrated *coup d'état* denounced the leaders as conspirators, tore up the proposed constitution and formed a new committee composed of those sympathetic to the Pankhurst doctrine.

The following extract written by Billington-Greig soon after the split certainly expresses a deep hostility towards the Pankhursts. But it also confirms some historians' views that the Pankhurst leadership dealt with criticism by ignoring it.

1   When the Conference day came it was attended by delegates and individual members indiscriminately who assembled ready for discussion on constructive lines. But instead of discussion, there was an announcement of dictatorship put forward with all the eloquence, skill and feel-
5   ing of which Mrs Pankhurst was capable. The draft Constitution was dramatically torn up and thrown to the ground. The assembled members were informed that they were in the ranks in an army of which she was the permanent Commander-in-Chief.

In response to the rejection of the Constitution, Teresa Billington-Greig and Charlotte Despard, along with a fifth of the WSPU membership, left to found the Women's Freedom League (WFL). 'If we are fighting against the subjection of woman to man, we cannot honestly submit to the subjection of woman to woman,' said Teresa Billington-Greig.[16]

However, the WFL failed to establish any distinctive image as in many ways it was a hybrid of the WSPU and the NUWSS. On the one hand it was a militant society, engaging in illegal actions, but on the other hand it was democratic and thus it fell between the law-breaking suffragettes and the law-abiding suffragists. Furthermore, although the WFL was supposedly non-party it remained loyal to its Labour origins, worked closely with local Labour groups and campaigned for Labour candidates at elections. Interestingly, the WFL too was often beset by internal divisions so that even the rebellious Billington-Greig came to envy the alleged autocratic style of the WSPU.

Friendship ties were swiftly broken whenever the Pankhursts were criticised. Emmeline and Frederick Pethick-Lawrence, who were Christabel's close friends, were expelled from the WSPU in October 1912. The Pethick-Lawrences had not only questioned the escalation of violence but Fred, as the only man ever to take a large part in the running of the WSPU, was increasingly seen as a misfit in an all-female organisation. When Christabel Pankhurst announced that she 'disapproved of men's intimate concern' in the movement it augured badly for Fred's future role within the WSPU. In a remarkable token of generosity, the Pethick-Lawrences left the WSPU without acrimony, continued to publish Votes for Women and helped found the United Suffragists in early 1914, re-establishing links with the radical section of the Labour movement.

Family bonds, too, collapsed in the event of disagreement. In January 1914 Sylvia Pankhurst was summoned to Paris by her sister Christabel – who was in voluntary exile there (see page 87) – to be informed that she must either 'toe the line' or sever all links with the WSPU. Christabel informed her that the WSPU must have only one policy, one programme, and one command: those who wished to give an independent lead, or carry out programmes that differed from those laid down by the WSPU must create an independent organisation of their own. Moreover, Christabel Pankhurst disliked her sister's emphasis on class politics. In concentrating her energies in the East End of London, in conducting the campaign for votes for women along class lines and in forming a 'People's Army' to fight against class oppression, Sylvia Pankhurst was thought to discredit the WSPU. And because both sides refused to compromise the ELFS ceased to be a branch of the WSPU and became a separate organisation. This split may have permitted Sylvia Pankhurst the freedom to pursue her own politics but, cut off from the funds of the WSPU, the ELFS did not develop into a significant suffrage organisation. Nonetheless, Sylvia founded her own paper, the Woman's Dreadnought, and continued to concentrate on working-class women's suffrage.

Unlike the NUWSS, the WSPU did not publish information about its membership so it is difficult to calculate membership numbers. There is no doubt that its membership grew rapidly. The 'At Home' attendances in London rose to about 1000 each week and by 1910 its income was £33,027. This enabled the WSPU to employ 98 women office workers in London and 26 officers in charge of regional districts. The circulation of Votes for Women also increased to just under 40,000. However, in 1913 the wealth of the WSPU declined and it became clear that the success of its regional organisation was diminishing: 34 of its 88 branches were situated in London.

EMMELINE PANKHURST 1858–1928   *-Profile-*

Emmeline was born on 15 July 1858 in Manchester to Robert and Sophia Goulden. She was introduced to politics by her parents. As a young girl Emmeline collected money to help the American anti-slavery campaigns, attended the first suffrage meeting held in Manchester and met most of the radical activists of the period. In 1879 she married Richard Pankhurst, a leading barrister, and gave birth to five children. As a wife and mother (and later widow) she was a political activist of some distinction: she was a Poor Law Guardian, a member of the Manchester School Board, a founding member of the Manchester Independent Labour Party and was active in four different suffrage societies before she founded the WSPU.

In 1903, frustrated at the slow pace of the existing women's suffrage movement, she founded the Women's Social and Political Union (WSPU), which adopted a confrontational style of politics. By 1914, the WSPU was notorious for its militant actions: breaking windows, destroying golf-courses and blowing-up buildings. As leader of the WSPU, Emmeline Pankhurst was held responsible for the crimes committed by its members, especially when she claimed that 'I have advised, I have incited, I have conspired ... I accept the responsibility for it'. Not surprisingly, the Government constantly summonsed, arrested, tried and imprisoned her.

Emmeline Pankhurst's Convictions

February 1908	6 weeks for obstruction
October 1908	3 months for inciting the public to rush the House of Commons: released before sentence expired
Nov 1910	Arrested in Downing Street but no charge made
March 1912	2 months for property damage but never imprisoned
May 1912	9 months for conspiracy: released after 5 weeks
April 1913	5 years penal servitude

By 1914 Emmeline Pankhurst was refusing to eat, drink or sleep when she was imprisoned and walked up and down 'her cell until her legs gave out and when she could walk no longer she propped her body up against he cold stones and forced herself to keep awake'. Imprisonment, exacerbated by hunger strikes, weakened Emmeline Pankhurst. During her 3-day imprisonment in mid-July 1914 she 'lost almost a stone in weight. She suffered greatly from nausea and gastric disturbances and was released in a toxic conditions with a high temperature and a very intermittent pulse'. By this time she was in such a weak and exhausted condition, and was experiencing a great deal of cardiac discomfort and poor digestion that she had to be transported everywhere by ambulance. The Government, fearful of public criticism, never force-fed Emmeline Pankhurst but released her from prison when her health was critical and she had the 'odour of malnutrion' about her.

With the outbreak of the First World War Emmeline Pankhurst ceased campaigning for the vote and instead worked closely with her former enemy, Lloyd George, to recruit women munition workers, prevent strikes and promote the war effort in Russia, Canada and America. After the war when a partial vote was won she continued, as she had done before the suffragette movement, to be involved in other forms of political action. In the early 1920s, and in her sixties, Emmeline Pankhurst became a national figure in Canadian politics leading a campaign to prevent venereal diseases. When she eventually returned to England in 1926 she was adopted as Conservative candidate for the working-class district of Whitechapel.

4 Conclusion

KEY ISSUE How far was the suffrage movement divided?

By the outbreak of the First World War it seemed as if the suffrage movement was divided into two major camps: the suffragists and the suffragettes. However, such an analysis is misleading. Certainly, at leadership level there were distinct differences between the two groups but this was not the case among the general membership. As Sandra Holton has shown, many suffrage supporters joined both a militant and a constitutionalist society, paid two membership fees, attended two sets of meetings and campaigned for both groups. Such women may not have seen the suffrage movement as made up of antagonistic groups vying for members but as one movement with a common aim. Nonetheless, the two organisations were distinct. Undoubtedly, the NUWSS was the more democratic of the two, but we need to consider the signifiance of this in the heady atmosphere of Edwardian politics. Democracy is time-consuming: leadership has to be elected; votes have to be canvassed; and policies have to be discussed. It could be argued that the emphasis by the NUWSS on internal politics hindered direct action. In stark contrast, the WSPU spent little time discussing policy: in the immortal words of Emmeline Pankhurst, 'Deeds not Words' were paramount. Yet, of course, a group that campaigns for democracy but then does not practise it can be accused of a certain duplicity.

Although these two groups have dominated the historiography of the suffrage movement there were many other societies that have either yet to be researched or are under-researched. Professional women founded their own suffrage societies: the Artists' Franchise League, the Actresses' Franchise League, the London Graduates' League and the Scottish Universities Women's Suffrage Union were amongst them. Similarly different religious denominations set up suffrage groups: the Catholic Women's Suffrage Society, the Church League for Women's Suffrage, the Free Church League, the Friends' League and the Jewish League represented women from a variety of religious backgrounds. Women even set up suffrage organisations that reflected their political affiliations, such as the Conservative and Unionist Women's Franchise Association. From this list it seems as if most women were able to join a suffrage group that represented their profession, religion or political affiliation. However, the membership of these groups may have over-lapped with the two national bodies.

More importantly, despite the recent publication of a few excellent books (see page 138), there is still too little information about the suffrage movement in Ireland, Scotland and Wales. It is known that the NUWSS and the WSPU had active branches all over Scotland and Wales, whereas there were several Irish independent organisations: one of the most influential was the Irish Women's Franchise League (IWFL) founded in 1908. The lack of research on these groups raises wider historical questions about the Anglocentrism (where everything is considered in terms of England) of historians who have generally ignored the suffrage movement in the rest of the British Isles. It also raises questions about whether or not female unity was able to rise above national identity: the IWFL was formed because Irish women, like many of their male compatriots, had no desire to be led by Englishwomen. Unfortunately, the limited amount of published work on the suffrage movement outside England means that it is hard to make any worthwhile judgement.

The formation of so many different suffrage societies and the many divisions that occurred within them raise further questions about female solidarity. The suffrage movement, although a woman's movement, seemed to be little different from other reform groups in that it was characterised by political bickering and internal wrangling. In many ways, despite their negative comments, historians tend to have higher expectations of women than they do of men and are surprised when women – often assumed to be more co-operative and conciliatory – disagree in such a forthright manner. As a consequence, the splits, particularly within the WSPU, are unsympathetically portrayed as female squabbles rather than as serious political differences between intelligent participants.

Socialist historians have undoubtedly corrected the stereotypical image of the female suffragist as a middle-class spinster. They have shown that a significant number of working-class women, particularly in the north of England, participated in the suffrage movement. These findings certainly add a 'politically correct' respectability to the suffrage movement, but is it true? There is far too little known about the composition of the suffrage movement at grassroots level, and until historians build up a national picture based upon local research it will be impossible to gauge the extent of working-class support. Certainly at leadership level, the middle classes dominated. Suffrage leaders were usually married to wealthy men or belonged to wealthy families and were undeniably middle or upper middle class. In a political movement that relied upon the unpaid work of women, only those who were economically independent or married to men who were financially secure could afford to engage in political action. For example, the nineteenth-century suffragist Lydia Becker was able to devote her life to the suffrage cause because she was not expected to engage in paid work. Similarly, Barbara Bodichon, the daughter of a wealthy radical MP, enjoyed a generously endowed independent income. In the twentieth century, Lady Constance Lytton and Emmeline Pethick Lawrence were wealthy enough not only to support themselves but also to donate large sums of money to the WSPU. Most male political organisations – be they socialist or Conservative – have also been led by the middle class, but historians are not so critical of the class composition of even revolutionary groups. In contrast, historians seem obsessed about the class background of women's groups and one must ask – rather provocatively perhaps – why this is so.

The suffrage movement also had its female opponents. Some women disagreed with votes for women and campaigned against it. In 1889, Mrs Humphrey Ward persuaded 104 prominent women to sign an appeal against female suffrage. Indeed, female antipathy to the vote led to the formation of the Women's National Anti-Suffrage League in 1908. Most women were probably more apathetic than antagonistic towards votes for women. Membership of the suffrage movement may have been large but the majority of women did not belong to any suffrage group.

Despite schisms and irreconcilable differences the women's suffrage movement became a powerful political force within Victorian and Edwardian Britain. By 1914, largely because of its intensive campaigning, it had forced women's suffrage onto the agenda of all the political parties and had made votes for women one of the foremost issues facing the governing Liberal Party.

References

1 'Anne Knight and the Radical Subculture' by Gail Malmgreen, *Quaker History* (1982) p. 108.
2 *The Graphic*, December 1891 (I am indebted to Mrs Good and the late Mr Good for this source reference).
3 Women's Franchise League leaflet (LSU archive M50/2/32/1).
4 Letter from Lil Ashworth Hallett to M G Fawcett, May 1891 (WFL collection (M50/2/1/141LSU).
5 Letter from Ursula Bright to Emmeline Pankhurst, 27 Nov 1893 (Sylvia Pankhurst papers).
6 See *Feminism and Democracy*, Sandra Stanley Holton (Cambridge University Press, 1986) for an exploration of these ideas.
7 *Harriot Stanton Blatch and the Winning of Woman Suffrage*, Ellen Carol Dubois (Yale University Press, 1997), p. 70. See also 'From Anti-Slavery to Suffrage Militancy' by Sandra Stanley Holton in *Suffrage and Beyond*, Melanie Nolan (London: Pluto Press, 1994).
8 *The Cause*, Ray Strachey (Virago Press, 1978), p. 310.
9 'Christabel Pankhurst: Reclaiming her Power' by Elizabeth Sarah in *Feminist Theories*, Dale Spender (Woman's Press, 1987), pp. 261–2.
10 *Prudent Revolutionaries*, Brian Harrison (Clarendon Press, 1987) p. 41.
11 WSPU Annual Report (1908) p. 7.
12 *Rise Up Women: The Militant Campaign of the WSPU 1903–1914*, Andrew Rosen (Routledge and Kegan Paul, 1974) p. 77.
13 This is a brilliant article that challenges the idea that the WSPU became increasingly Conservative. 'Incipient toryism'? The Women's Social and Political Union and the Independent Labour Party, 1903–1914 by Krista Cowman, *History Workshop Journal*, Spring, 2002.
14 *Sylvia Pankhurst*, Barbara Winslow (UCL Press, 1996), p. 41.
15 *Feminist Theories*, Elizabeth Sarah (Women's Press, 1983) p. 270.
16 *Prudent Revolutionaries*, Brian Harrison (Clarendon Press, 1987) p. 50.

Summary Diagram
Similarities and differences in the suffrage movement

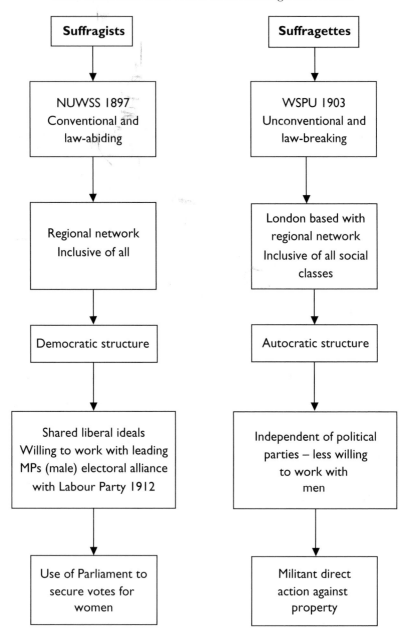

Working on Chapter 3

This chapter covers a great deal of information about the development of the various suffrage organisations of this period. You will not have to remember all the various splinter groups but you should be aware that the disagreements could be seen as healthy because they helped to shape future policy. You need to understand why the disagreements emerged and their implications for future actions by the NUWSS and the WSPU. To help you understand how these differences occurred you may find it useful to keep the following questions in mind. How did these groups differ organisationally? Why did the composition of the membership of each group differ? Was the suffrage movement really middle class?

Answering structured and essay questions on Chapter 3

Many of the questions on the topic covered in this chapter will revolve around why women felt the need to gain the vote and the methods they adopted to achieve their goals. Structured questions will usually consist of a number of questions with the final one carrying the highest mark. Consider the following examples:

1 **a)** Why was the 1867 Reform Bill so important in the development of the women's suffrage movement? (*8 marks*)
   b) Describe the stages in the formation of the NUWSS in the years 1867–97. (*12 marks*)
2 **a)** To what extent was the WSPU dominated by the Pankhurst family in the years 1903–14? (*8 marks*)
   b) Why did the Women's Social and Political Union resort to increased militancy in the years 1906–14? (*12 marks*)

Examiners will award low marks to essays that use a narrative approach, and/or do not answer the question directly. They are looking for the ability to construct a relevant argument; in the case of the Pankhursts' domination of the WPSU, does the evidence presented in this chapter suggest reasons for or against this proposition? Questions are structured in such a way that they offer you the opportunity to construct an argument, which may well challenge the view expressed, although it is totally acceptable to agree with the view if you think this correct.

Questions on the growth of the women's suffrage movement tend to focus on:

a) The influence of the Great Reform Bills on women
b) The divisions and splits within the women's suffrage movement
c) The impact of the different methods adopted by the NUWSS and WSPU.

A typical question is:

> Was the argument over the principle of women's enfranchisement won by the time the Pankhursts joined the campaign for female suffrage?

Write down the achievements made by the NUWSS before the emergence of the Pankhursts. Discuss the reasons for and against why the NUWSS had failed to gain the vote. Then consider what contributions the Pankhursts made and to what extent they hindered or furthered the cause of women and the right to vote.

Answering source-based questions on Chapter 3

Read carefully the *Votes for Working Women* extract from *The Suffragette* on page 44 and then answer the following questions:

a) Explain briefly the reference: Mr Lloyd George in particular has held out the hope that 'millions of women' will be enfranchised in this way. (*4 marks*)

b) In what ways does the cartoon reinforce the role of working women in the struggle for the vote? (*6 marks*)

c) How useful is this source to an historian enquiring into the influence of the suffragettes on working women? (*8 marks*)

d) To what extent was the women's suffrage movement a class-based one? (*12 marks*)

The Suffrage Campaigns

POINTS TO CONSIDER

The main question to consider in this chapter is to what extent the suffrage movement can be divided into two completely separate groups: militant and non-militant, suffragettes and suffragists. You should be able to understand the reasons for militancy and begin to form your own opinions as to whether or not violence ever succeeds. By the end of the chapter you should have some understanding of the variety of methods used by both suffragists and suffragettes.

KEY DATES

1866 First women's suffrage petition presented to Parliament; first public meeting on women's suffrage held in London

1867 Two women's suffrage petitions presented to Parliament; campaign to get women's names on the electoral register

1868 *Chorlton* v. *Ling* case

1870 *Women's Suffrage Journal* published; Quaker women had property confiscated for refusing to pay taxes

1874 First suffrage meeting held in Manchester

1905 Christabel Pankhurst and Annie Kenney arrested for causing a disturbance

1906 WSPU by-election policy established

1907 First Women's Parliament at Caxton Hall established by WSPU; *Votes for Women* published; demonstration organised by NUWSS

1908 First window-smashing and chaining to railings; joint suffrage demonstration; WFL members chain themselves to grille in House of Commons; *Common Cause* published

1909 Deputations to Parliament by WFL and WSPU; Woman's Exhibition; hunger strike

1910 Conciliation Bill truce until Black Friday; joint WSPU and WFL demonstration

1911 Coronation Year: suffragettes resume truce; WFL and WSPU boycott census; united suffrage demonstration

1912 Mass window-smashing; attempted arson; letter box damage begins; NUWSS-Labour Party alliance established

1913 Golf courses ruined; telegraph wires cut; arson attacks; Emily Davison dies after injuries sustained on Derby Day; protest chanting begins in churches; *Suffragette* published

1914 Rokeby Venus slashed; suffragette demonstration to Buckingham Palace; militancy ceases when war is declared

1 Introduction

> **KEY ISSUE** Can one divide the women's suffrage movement into
> suffragists and suffragettes?

In February 1913 suffragettes smashed a jewellery case in the Tower
of London, destroyed hundreds of orchids in Kew Gardens, damaged
several golf courses and placed a bomb in Lloyd George's house at
Walton Heath. The story of the few militant suffragettes who were willing to do such deeds has gained almost legendary status. These were
women who were prepared to sacrifice their friends, family and –
sometimes – their lives to win the vote. However, the historian needs
to challenge some of the assumptions that accompany it. There are at
least two widely held beliefs that need to be questioned. The first, and
probably the more important, concerns the difference in political
strategies between the suffragists and the suffragettes. In popular
belief, the suffragists are assumed to be conventional and law-abiding,
whereas the suffragettes have acquired the image of being unconventional and law-breaking. Indeed, the women's suffrage movement is
seen to be split between those (like the National Union of Women's
Suffrage Societies, the NUWSS) who favoured moral force and those
(like the Women's Social and Political Union, the WSPU) who
favoured physical force. At first, it is generally argued, the methods
used by all the suffrage groups were peaceful – and legal – but as time
went on more violent – and illegal – methods were favoured, particularly by the WSPU. As a consequence the suffragists are usually
regarded as constitutional, the suffragettes as militant. However, this
division needs examining. In a thought-provoking essay Sandra Holton
suggests it is important to overcome the 'analytical imprecision' of the
term 'militant'.[1] Militancy is an elastic concept that changed its meaning over the 50 or more years in which women campaigned for the
vote: suffragists were considered militant in 1860 when they dared to
speak at meetings but by 1914 public speaking was seen to be quite
acceptable female behaviour.

The second question concerns the relationship between the suffragists and the suffragettes. It is assumed, erroneously, that – because
of the differences over political tactics – there was hostility between
the various women's suffrage organisations. The NUWSS were said to
be antagonistic towards the WSPU because its members used violent
methods, whereas the WSPU were said to condemn the NUWSS's lack
of imagination. This interpretation too needs to be reassessed, as the
NUWSS initially condoned the militancy of the WSPU and held ban-
quets in honour of those who had been imprisoned. The Criterion
Restaurant in Piccadilly, London, was even hired to host welcoming
parties for women who had just been released from gaol. This support
was not to last. The increasingly violent tactics of the WSPU gradually

alienated the NUWSS and by 1909 it was voicing public disapproval of the WSPU's tactics. Nevertheless, the divisions between the two groups were not always constant. For example, when the WSPU called a temporary halt to militancy (which, apart from a brief lapse in November 1910, lasted from January 1910 to November 1911) the old spirit of unity reappeared and the suffrage groups organised joint meetings and demonstrations.

2 Legal Methods

> **KEY ISSUE** Campaigners for the suffrage tried a great range of approaches and methods to publicise their cause and win support. Which of these methods do you consider were most likely to be effective?

Between 1860 and 1914 various methods were used to publicise the issue of votes for women. For most of this time both the suffragists and suffragettes generally used peaceful and legitimate measures copied from other reform groups. Early suffragists learned a lot about political tactics from their participation in the Anti-Corn Law campaigns of the early nineteenth century. They discovered how to organise public meetings, demonstrate, write propaganda literature, raise money, lobby MPs and petition Parliament – all traditional middle-class methods of persuasive campaigning. Although the WSPU later adopted a confrontational style they continued to combine more traditional methods with the new.

a) Meetings

All the women's suffrage groups held both semi-private and public meetings to generate publicity and recruit members. Guests were invited to meetings at people's houses to listen to speakers on questions concerning women. Public meetings, initially advertised for women only, were also organised. Lydia Becker and other suffrage workers spoke at mothers' meetings, church groups and political organisations to publicise women's suffrage. The NUWSS raised the question of women's suffrage at trade union conferences and visited most of the major cotton towns to publicise the cause. Public meetings were also organised by the WSPU throughout the country to consolidate support, gain recruits, collect money and sell papers. In 1909, for instance, large meetings were held in the Royal Albert Hall and the Queen's Hall, London; the Colston Hall, Bristol; the Sun Hall, Liverpool; the Albert Hall, Nottingham; the Town Hall, Birmingham; the Synod Hall, Edinburgh; St Andrew's Hall, Glasgow; and the Rotunda, Dublin. Such meetings were carefully orchestrated and planned. In Birmingham, the WSPU divided the city into districts, each with an organiser who had to co-ordinate four small weekly meetings to publicise women's suffrage. The WSPU broke new organisational ground by speaking to audiences in the open air at places such as Trafalgar Square, Blackheath Common and village greens throughout the country. Supporters soon became used to suffragettes speaking wherever women were to be found in large numbers: the local market squares, bus and tram stations, factory gates, shops and even breweries. However as photographs taken at the time show, women did not always attend. By the beginning of the twentieth century both the WSPU and the NUWSS were even holding meetings at fairs and wakes to publicise the cause. One of the most important meetings held by the WSPU took place in London. On 13 February 1907 the WSPU held what they called the first Women's Parliament at Caxton Hall, just across the square from the House of Commons, as a protest against their exclusion from the franchise. Suffrage meetings such as these often attracted large audiences. In 1880, one suffrage speaker filled the Manchester Free Trade Hall with women who had walked up to 20 miles to attend. When Emmeline Pankhurst spoke there many years later she too addressed a huge number of women.

Some considered these early suffragists daring and unladylike on the grounds that it was unseemly for women to speak in public.

Suffragettes at Torquay Regatta.

Victorian society was profoundly shocked when Millicent Fawcett and another suffragist spoke to a mixed audience at the Architectural Society in London in 1869. One MP even mentioned the incident in Parliament: he referred to two ladies who had recently disgraced themselves but would not mention their names in case it caused further embarrassment. However, by the end of the nineteenth century public speaking had generally become unexceptional unless it took place at an unusual event. For instance, in 1908, when Millicent Fawcett became the first woman to debate at the Oxford Union, she once again received a great deal of publicity.

b) Demonstrations and Pilgrimages

Demonstrations, a typical expression of protest by pressure groups, were common to all the suffrage organisations because they could draw members together in a feeling of communal identity, engender a sense of purpose and publicise votes for women. The first of the big suffrage demonstrations, organised by the NUWSS, took place in February 1907 and became known as the Mud March because of the torrential rain that poured down on the demonstrators. Even as late as 1907 it was considered unladylike to participate in outdoor protest, so the 3000 or more women who marched from Hyde Park Corner risked their reputation and sometimes their employment. However, despite the rain, the demonstration was considered a great success. In 1908, Emmeline Pankhurst, determined not to be outdone, led the first of the WSPU's large-scale demonstrations where seven different processions met in Hyde Park. In 1910 the WSPU and the WFL organised another, which was even bigger and better. Here, Emmeline Pankhurst headed a column of over 600 ex-prisoners, each carrying a prison arrow. In 1911 a London Coronation march, held in honour of the new King, George V, was organised by all the suffrage societies and drew approximately 40,000 demonstrators. A month-long pilgrimage from Edinburgh to London in 1912 also drew thousands of supporters. Similarly a pilgrimage in August 1913 organised by the NUWSS (from all parts of Britain to the capital city) enjoyed great success. Demonstrators were greeted by bands and provided with food and drink throughout their journeys.

The WSPU gave demonstrations a new direction as, with impressive skill, they introduced a touch of melodrama to an old form of protest. Some of the members of the WSPU were great extroverts and livened up demonstrations by making them into dramatic performances. As Diane Atkinson has pointed out,[2] the black and white photographs of this period do not reveal the fact that the movement was extremely colourful. When Emmeline Pethick-Lawrence selected the colours of purple for dignity, white for purity and green for hope to represent the suffragettes, she created a potent symbol. Suffragettes proudly wore these colours in public. They certainly dressed up to

The NUWSS at Hyde Park.

take part in demonstrations: in plain white with sashes of purple, white and green; in the costumes of famous women (Joan of Arc was a popular figure); in their working clothes (as pit brow women, factory workers, doctors, teachers); in their national costume or carrying national flags (Scottish women wore tartan, Irish women carried flags and were accompanied by Irish pipers); and as ex-prisoners (dressed in prison clothes). Demonstrators carried 8-feet-high banners and enormous posters with the portraits of the leadership on them. Various bands, including a suffragette drum-and-fife band dressed in WSPU colours, accompanied these bright and dazzling processions. Hence one historian has called these events 'the spectacle of women'.

c) Propaganda Techniques

Throughout this period, all the various suffrage groups developed lively propaganda to promote votes for women. In 1867 Lydia Becker wrote an article called 'Female Suffrage'. This was published in a leading periodical, *Contemporary Review*, and subsequently printed and sold as a pamphlet. Suffrage groups published their own newspapers and wrote their own plays, short stories and poems. The regular production of suffrage newspapers, such as *The Women's Suffrage Journal* from 1870, *Votes for Women* from 1907, the *Common Cause* from 1909 and *The Suffragette* from 1913 proved to be a valuable means of both publicising the women's suffrage cause and of keeping the various groups and associations in touch with one another.

The Actresses' Franchise League wrote and performed propaganda plays in drawing rooms and public theatres in order to strengthen supporters and make converts. In these plays, the female was generally portrayed as a heroine pitted against an unyielding and intransigent male. One popular play called *The Reforming of Augustus* concerned the conversion of an antagonistic male to women's suffrage as a result of a dream. Plays such as *How the Vote Was Won* written by Elizabeth Robins, a distinguished dramatist and an active member of the WSPU, were performed to sympathetic audiences throughout Britain.

Suffragettes even disrupted plays about female heroines. On one occasion three suffragettes barricaded themselves into a box at Covent Garden to interrupt a production of *Joan of Arc*. Their aim was to draw similarities between the treatment of Joan and the treatment of the suffragettes at the hands of a hostile government. A film called *True Womanhood* was about the struggle for women's suffrage, and music, poetry and limericks were also used to make the political point. *The March of the Women*, the rallying song for the WSPU, had a catchy tune and memorable lyrics. On the 10 February 1911 a poem entitled *Woman This, and Woman That*, written by Laurence Housman, was recited outside Woolwich Town Hall to an audience of hundreds:

1   We went before a magistrate who would not hear us speak;
    To a drunken brute who beat his wife he only gave a week:
    But we were sent to Holloway a calendar month or more,
    Because we dared, against his will, to knock at Asquith's door.

5   When women go to work for them the Government engage
    To give them lots of contract jobs at a low starvation wage;
    But when it's men that they employ they always add a note –
    'Fair wages must be paid' – because the men have got the vote.

    You talk of sanitation, and temperance, and schools,
10 And you send your male inspectors to impose your man-made rules;
    'The woman's sphere's the home' you say? then prove it to our face;
    Give us the vote that we may make the home a happier place!

The WSPU, as Diane Atkinson has pointed out, were great saleswomen. They designed, advertised and marketed a wide variety of goods in their London shops. Tea Caddies, soap, cakes and even the ubiquitous stock cube were designed for sale in the suffragette colours. Cards, crackers, jewellery, suffragette dolls, scarves in various shades of purple, white summer blouses, badges, bags and belts were all sold in the WSPU shops. Books, pamphlets and leaflets, stationery, games and playing cards were also on display. Bazaars were organised to raise money and to win support. At one bazaar in Glasgow, which raised over £1700, a quilt embroidered with the names of suffragette hunger strikers was offered for sale. At the Women's Exhibition and Sale of Work in Knightsbridge in 1909 a photographic history of the suffrage movement, a reproduction of a prison cell and plays performed by the Actresses Franchise League entertained – and educated – the vast numbers who attended. In the 2 weeks in which the exhibition was open it collected £6000 and recruited over 200 women.

Some of the methods used in the early twentieth century, particularly by the WSPU, suggest a playfulness and sense of humour that was far removed from the conventional dour image of the suffrage movement. The WSPU was highly innovative in its propaganda techniques, rarely missing an opportunity to promote votes for women. Groups of cyclists went out regularly on bicycles decorated with the suffragette colours to advertise demonstrations. At the 1908 Football Cup Final, held at Crystal Palace in London, the WSPU distributed envelopes with the teams' colours on them inviting the wives of the male spectators to meetings. On the day of the match they flew a kite with 'Votes for Women' written on it above the pitch and distributed suffragette leaflets at nearby railway stations. At one of the boat races between Oxford and Cambridge, the WSPU ran a launch filled with 'Votes for Women' banners, while on another occasion it hired a boat to sail to the House of Commons in order to harangue MPs taking tea on the terrace. One member of the Women's Freedom League even hired a balloon to fly across London to drop leaflets supporting votes for women.

d) Persuading Parliament

As only Parliament had the constitutional right to grant the vote to women, suffragists tried desperately to convince MPs of the logic of women's suffrage. At first, conventional middle-class methods of pressure were used: the legality of women's exclusion from the vote was tested, Parliament was petitioned and MPs were lobbied. It was the politics of persuasion rather than the politics of confrontation.

Petitioning the House of Commons was a time-honoured way of publicising reform issues. The Anti-Corn League had successfully used this method and it was favoured not only because it indicated to the Government that large numbers were in favour of votes for women but because it helped arouse public interest in the campaign. But women of course were without the vote and their petitions were not received with as much sympathy as those of the men who petitioned against the Corn Laws of the early nineteenth century. Suffragists were familiar with the methods of other protest groups and, as Martin Pugh points out in *The March of the Women*, the use of petitions was a tribute to the memory of the huge Chartist petitions of an earlier period. In 1866 Emily Davies and Elizabeth Garrett delivered a petition containing 1499 signatures to John Stuart Mill who promised to present it to Parliament. In 1867 two petitions were presented to the House of Commons to convince MPs of the popularity of Mill's proposed amendment to a men's suffrage Bill being debated. The amendment would have extended the vote to women. Large petitions also gained publicity especially when Emily Davies sent copies of one petition to 500 newspapers.

In the 1860s suffragists attempted to use the legal system to gain the vote. In 1867 a widowed shop-keeper named Mrs Lily Maxwell had been mistakenly put on the electoral register and went to cast her vote publicly on the hustings accompanied by a large number of suffrage supporters. Her vote was accepted and inspired over 5000 other female house-holders to do the same. Eventually, in 1868 in a case known technically as the *Chorlton* v. *Lings* case the High Court examined the validity of the women's claims. Sir John Coleridge and Richard Pankhurst represented the women, both arguing that women had once enjoyed the right to vote but had been excluded in the 1832 Great Reform Act. It was also argued that the general term MAN that had been used in the 1832 Act included women. A similar case, *Brown* v. *Ingram*, took place in Scotland but both the English and the Scottish petitioners lost when the Courts refused to accept the validity of their claim. Suffragists also lobbied MPs to gain their support for women's suffrage. In June 1887 Lydia Becker formed the first Committee of Members of Parliament who pledged their commitment to votes for women. A total of 71 MPs joined. As a result of the combined work of this Committee and the NUWSS, a private member's bill in support of women's suffrage was brought in almost every year. In addition, efforts were made to amend government franchise bills to include women's suffrage. In 1867 John Stuart Mill introduced the first ever women's suffrage amendment to the Second Reform Bill while William Woodall, a Liberal MP for Stoke on Trent, tried to secure the inclusion of a woman's suffrage amendment to the Third Reform Bill of 1884. The three Plural voting Bills of 1906, 1913 and 1914 and the 1912 Irish Home Rule Bill each had an amendment attached in support of votes for women. All of the amendments failed.

In the late nineteenth and early twentieth century suffragists worked hard to elect Liberal MPs who supported votes for women. It was common practice for the NUWSS to canvass votes for sympathetic Liberal MPs at general elections and by-elections. In 1906 Wigan textile workers canvassed at by-elections for MPs who supported women's suffrage and in 1907 the NUWSS adopted a similar approach in Hexham, Jarrow, Kirkdale and Wimbledon. In Wimbledon the NUWSS ran the entire election campaign of the women's suffrage candidate. In the 1910 general election the Birmingham branch of the NUWSS wrote to 52 parliamentary candidates to obtain their views on women's suffrage, undertook door-to-door canvassing to support sympathisers and picketed the election booths.

Until the Liberal landslide of 1906 the NUWSS concentrated much of its energies on opposing Conservative candidates. However, the Liberal victory left the NUWSS with a political dilemma. Although the Liberals brought women's suffrage no further forward, suffragists had no wish to embarrass a government that so many of them supported and to which many of their male relatives belonged. By 1910, however, the patience of the NUWSS had worn thin and it became official NUWSS policy to run suffrage candidates against opponents from all of the major political parties, including the Liberals.

From 1912 onwards the NUWSS, disillusioned by what they perceived as the continuing duplicity of the Liberal Party, redirected their allegiance to the Labour Party. It subsidised Labour MPs in Parliament who were sympathetic to women's suffrage and set up an Election Fighting Fund to defeat the Liberals. These tactics were, by and large, successful. In the last by-election campaign supported by the Election Fighting Fund (fought in Midlothian, Scotland, in 1912), the NUWSS claimed that the Liberals had been defeated because their Labour candidate had taken away valuable Liberal votes.

e) Harassing Authority

The WSPU came to prefer confrontation to the politics of persuasion, believing that they could force the government to grant women the vote. The first incident occurred in 1905 during an election campaign when Christabel Pankhurst and Annie Kenney interrupted Sir Edward Grey and Winston Churchill at a meeting in Manchester's Free Trade Hall. During a pause in questions, Annie Kenney asked Churchill 'If you are elected, will you do your best to make Women's Suffrage a Government measure?' When no reply was given, Christabel Pankhurst held up a banner entitled 'Votes for Women'. At this moment, the lecture theatre erupted and when order was restored the Chief Constable of Manchester suggested putting the question in writing. Edward Grey and Churchill, both of whom paid lip service to women's suffrage, refused to answer the question. Just as the meeting was to be adjourned Annie Kenney unfurled a banner asking for votes for women and shouted 'Will the Liberal Government give women the vote?' The banner display and Annie Kenney's interruption caused further uproar and stewards and police evicted the two women from the hall. In response, Christabel Pankhurst spat in the face of at least two police officers and hit another. When Christabel and Annie Kenney attempted to address the crowd that had assembled outside the Hall, they were arrested, fined and charged with disorderly behaviour and obstruction. Christabel Pankhurst used the subsequent trial as a political platform stating that 'we cannot make any orderly protest because we have not the means whereby citizens may do such a thing; we have not a vote; and so long as we have not votes we must be disorderly'. They refused to pay the fine – or even accept the payment of the fine by Winston Churchill – and so were imprisoned.

This incident created what Christabel Pankhurst desired: much needed publicity for women's suffrage. Imprisonment was news. Protests at public meetings addressed by members of the Government proved to be a very successful means of calling attention to the demand for votes for women. A meeting (in the same Hall) organised by the WSPU to welcome the return of the militants was packed to capacity. The two who had been unceremoniously thrown out a week previously were now on the platform speaking to an audience prepared to listen carefully to what they had to say. Despite criticism from the press about the unladylike behaviour of Annie Kenney and Christabel Pankhurst, the WSPU began to attract sizeable audiences and perhaps, more importantly, enjoyed an increase in membership.

This sequence of events was to be re-enacted on numerous occasions as women interrupted government leaders, were arrested, refused to pay fines and were imprisoned and then received what was in essence free publicity and, as a consequence, increased membership. It was a heady formula for success. All the leaders of the Liberal Party – Churchill, Campbell-Bannerman, Asquith, Lloyd George and Edward Grey – suffered from WSPU heckling at their meetings, whether they supported women's suffrage or not. The WSPU interrupted political speeches when Liberal MPs were talking in support of women's suffrage because their leaders believed that these politicians were insincere. For example, Winston Churchill had his speeches interrupted because, as a senior member of the Liberal Government, he was held equally responsible for its refusal to grant women the vote. Similarly, in 1908 Lloyd George was heckled by WSPU members wearing prison uniforms when he gave a speech to a women's suffrage meeting sponsored by the WFL.

In a by-election at Cockermouth in 1906 Christabel initiated a policy of opposing Liberal party candidates in order to force the Government into taking the question of votes for women seriously. When the Liberal MP lost his seat at Cockermouth the WSPU were jubilant and from this time on, at every by-election where a Liberal candidate was in the field, members of the WSPU were present to urge the electorate to vote against him. They claimed their greatest success when Winston Churchill lost his seat at a Manchester by-election and was forced to flee to Dundee to fight another. At the same time, the politically neutral WSPU continued to cultivate the support of various MPs from the other two parties. Christabel Pankhurst corresponded privately with the former Conservative Prime Minister Arthur Balfour, to gain his support for votes for women, while Emmeline and Sylvia remained close to Keir Hardie and MPs from the Labour Party.

At first it was just the Liberal Party that suffered from interruptions, but in October 1912 the WSPU decided to oppose Labour Party MPs too. This was a calculated reaction to Labour's decision to pledge support to a Liberal government that force-fed women. When the government took the step of banning women from political meetings the WSPU's response was highly ingenious. Suffragettes concealed themselves between organ pipes or lurked under platforms. Some were lowered into political meetings at the end of ropes. When Winston Churchill, by now MP for Dundee, was due to speak at the

Kinnaird Hall in Dundee, suffragettes concealed themselves in a building nearby so that they could throw stones at the windows roof's skylight. Similarly, in Birmingham, two women climbed on the roof of a house to throw tiles on to Asquith, who was due to speak at a nearby hall. There are reports of politicians being harassed at golf clubs, outside churches and even outside their own homes.

Jane Marcus stresses the importance of the 'interruption of male political discourse'[2] in the suffrage campaign. The strategy of interrupting the speeches of male politicians, she suggests, marked a watershed in suffrage history. By stopping male politicians speaking, the suffragettes not only challenged male authority but claimed a political voice for women who were supposed to remain silent. Of course this is historical speculation: the WSPU perhaps had more pragmatic reasons for interrupting the Government. Indeed they were possibly more influenced by Parnell's obstructionist tactics in the Irish Home Rule campaign of the 1880s than in interrupting men to make a feminist point. Parnell heckled all Liberal candidates at elections whether or not they supported Home Rule because the Liberal Government was held responsible for the continuing colonisation of Ireland. The Pankhursts' were all too aware that Richard Pankhurst, who had stood for Parliament as a Liberal candidate and was a keen supporter of Home Rule, had been defeated in 1885 because of Irish opposition. If the WSPU could similarly embarrass the Liberal Government then the vote could not be far off – or so it was thought.

The WSPU also directed its energies towards disrupting what they regarded as the male authority of the church. They identified the church as an object of attack because it was seen paradoxically both as the 'lackey' of government and as a symbol of resistance against authority (see pages 92–3 for the church response to the suffrage movement). Either way, the suffragettes confronted the church with remarkable fervour and dedication. On the one hand, the church was condemned for its 'shameful and obsequiously compliant attitude'[3] in not speaking out against the perceived torture of imprisoned suffragette martyrs. Yet, on the other hand, the church was criticised because it denied the Christian doctrine of equality by not actively supporting votes for women. And largely because Jesus Christ was regarded as a rebel who spoke out against injustice, the church was thought to need reminding of its historical role in championing the oppressed. There were therefore widespread protests in various churches and cathedrals where suffragettes interrupted services to offer prayers in support of votes for women. For example, in 1913 at St Mary's Baptist Chapel in Norwich, a woman rose during the service to say 'Oh Lord Jesus, who dost at all times show tender compassion to women, hear now our petitions for our sisters who are being tortured in prison … by men calling themselves Christians.'[4] Annie Kenney even arrived with her luggage at Lambeth Palace to seek sanctuary from the Archbishop of Canterbury until the vote had been won, but after providing her with lunch and tea he called the police who promptly arrested her.

Despite the efforts of the suffragists and the somewhat alienating tactics of the suffragettes, votes for women seemed no further forward. As a consequence, the suffragettes turned to other forms of political action to get their voice heard. And it is this type of action that has aroused the most controversy.

3 Illegal Methods

KEY ISSUES Why did the WSPU turn to militancy? May WSPU militancy have undermined NUWSS peaceful persuasion?

a) Reasons for Increased Militancy

From 1908 the WSPU intensified the political pressure and promoted new and confrontational methods to force MPs to give women the vote. The reason for this turn to violence is open to debate. Unsympathetic observers have viewed militancy humourously or else sought explanations within a psychological framework of madness and abnormality. George Dangerfield, for example, writes comically about women:

> 1 It is almost impossible to write the story of the Woman's Rebellion
> without admitting certain elements of brutal comedy. From the spec-
> tacle of women attacking men there rises an outrageous, an unprinci-
> pled laughter. And when a scene as ordinary as English politics is
> 5 suddenly disturbed with the swish of long skirts, the violent assault of
> feathered hats, the impenetrable, advancing phalanx of corseted
> bosoms – when, around the smoking ruins of some house or church,
> there is discovered the dread evidence of a few hairpins or a feminine
> galosh – then the amazing, the ludicrous appearance of the whole thing
> 10 is almost irresistible.[5]

Militancy, for some anti-suffragists, was seen as a reflection of the widespread instability of women, and of their fanatical and hysterical tendencies in particular. To them, it was proof that women should not be allowed to vote. The first historians to comment on the suffragettes agreed with the anti-suffragists, emphasised the psychological weakness of the suffragettes and decried militancy as the action of a few demented spinsters. Some saw militancy as the sign of 'individual psychological imbalance' but later historians are critical of this interpretation and suggest that militancy was a rational response to male intransigence. Brian Harrison, for example, claims that militancy was a short-term tactical necessity born of the failure of legal and peaceful methods. Even so Harrison is not averse to trivialising the women's struggle: 'This inversion of society's values was by no means complete; it closely resembles the schoolgirls' surreptitious breaking of the rules when the headmistress is away rather than the revolutionary's contemptuous and frontal challenge to the established order.'[6] Radical feminist historians view suffragette violence quite differently. To their minds, violent behaviour challenged male supremacy, thus establishing the WSPU as not only heroic but as the precursor of modern feminism. Radical feminists may well take the violence of the WSPU seriously but the adoption of a Whiggish interpretation (whereby the WSPU is seen to have lain the foundation for women's emancipation) needs a more far-reaching analysis.

Suffragettes argued that violence emerged and escalated for a number of core reasons that served to justify it. Firstly, militancy was adopted in response to the failure of years of peaceful campaigning to which politicians were seen to have turned a deaf ear. Secondly, militancy was a reaction to the 1906 Liberal Government that, by excluding women from public meetings and refusing to meet suffrage deputations, had denied suffragettes the main forms of agitation open to the disenfranchised. Suffragettes, forbidden access to peaceful protest, believed that they were left with only one alternative: violence. Thirdly, militancy was seen as a retaliatory measure against a Government that imprisoned and force-fed those who participated in direct action (see pages 88–91). If the Government chose to treat women roughly then it too would be intimidated. Fourthly, suffragettes believed themselves to be continuing a long and venerable tradition of protest as previous extensions to the franchise, for instance in 1832 and 1867, had been preceded by great disturbances. The WSPU drew on historical examples of the unlawful exercise of physical force to justify its tactics and identified the suffragettes with past revolutionary and resistance heroes. One male supporter of votes for women remarked ironically:

1   Of course, when men wanted the franchise, they did not behave in the unruly manner of our feminine friends. They were perfectly constitutional in their agitation. In Bristol, I find they only burnt the Mansion House, the Custom House, the Bishop's Palace, the Excise Office, three
5   prisons, four tollhouses, and forty-two private dwellings and warehouses, all in a perfectly constitutional and respectable manner ... Four men were respectably hanged at Bristol and three in Nottingham ... In this and other ways the males set a splendid example of constitutional methods in agitating for the franchise.[7]

Finally, suffragettes had come to believe that the Government would not grant women the vote until they were forced to do so. Comparisons were drawn between the suffragettes and other pressure groups who advocated violent methods. Christabel Pankhurst, for instance, noted that miners had succeeded in gaining improved pay and conditions in 1911 because they made themselves a nuisance. Similarly the tactics of the Ulster Unionists, seen to go unchecked and unpunished even when it involved the loss of human life, were successful in stopping the move towards Irish Home Rule. The suffragettes believed that the achievements of these groups demonstrated that the vote would only be obtained through violent action.

The popular image of the militant is of an expensively dressed woman smashing windows in the main shopping streets of London. In fact the first illegal methods used were little more than mild forms of civil disobedience. Initially women tried to undermine the business of the government by refusing to support a state that refused them recognition. Two of the most common ways to achieve this were tax and census evasion.

b) Tax Evasion and Census Resistance

The refusal of women to pay their taxes had a long history in the annals of the suffrage movement, since from the beginning women were quick to claim that taxation and representation were inseparably united (see page 11). In 1870 two Quaker suffragists had their property seized by bailiffs when they refused to pay taxes. More than 35 years later Mrs Montefiore barricaded herself in her Hammersmith house in defiance of the bailiffs sent to seize her home for non-payment of tax. The Women's Freedom League, under the direction of Charlotte Despard, adopted a similar policy and described it as 'constitutional militancy'. A number of wealthy suffragists lost property and faced heavy fines for non-payment of taxes but continued to believe that the sacrifice was worthwhile.

All the suffrage groups linked the census with citizenship and citizenship with suffrage so that 'no-vote, no-census' became one of their rallying cries. Every 10 years, since 1801, the government organised an official count of the population – a census – in order to plan for the future. The Women's Freedom League organised a boycott of the 1911 census, and this was endorsed by the WSPU and the NUWSS. On 2 April 1911, the day of the census, large numbers of women made elaborate arrangements to be away from home for the night in order to avoid the census enumerator. Women with large houses offered overnight accommodation to those who were away from home. In Edinburgh a large cafe was hired by the WSPU so that women who wanted to evade the census had somewhere safe to stay. Others stayed in the WFL headquarters in Glasgow or the WSPU offices elsewhere, some went to the all-night entertainments put on by the various suffrage societies; and at least one member of the WFL spent the whole night on skates at the Aldwych Skating Rink!

c) Window Smashing

One of the WSPU's first violent tactics was breaking windows: an impromptu act borne of desperation rather than a coherent political strategy. The first window smashing began as a response to the treatment that women received outside the House of Commons in 1908. Asquith, the Prime Minister, had refused to receive a deputation of suffragettes who were subsequently treated with great brutality. Exasperated, Edith New and Mary Leigh smashed two windows at 10 Downing Street.

The next bout of window smashing occurred when Emmeline Pankhurst and a group of elderly suffragists were evicted from the House of Commons and arrested when trying to deliver a petition. This event prompted women to break windows at the Treasury and the Home Office in protest against such treatment. Once again, window breaking was not authorised by the WSPU leadership but was an angry and impassioned response to government intransigence and police violence. Yet window breaking soon gained retrospective approval from the leadership of the WSPU, and then it became official policy. When Mrs Pankhurst remarked that 'the argument of the broken window pane is the most valuable argument in modern politics', she endorsed the window smashers. Soon afterwards, the smashing of windows became part of a well-orchestrated campaign, with suffragettes travelling down from as far as Scotland to take part.[8] Even so, window smashing was generally used as a response to what they took to be government double-dealing. For instance, when Asquith rejected a Conciliation Bill for women's suffrage in November 1911 the WSPU membership reacted immediately by shattering windows at the Home Office, the War Office, the Foreign Office, the Board of Education, the Board of Trade, the Treasury, Somerset House, the National Liberal Club, Guards Club, the *Daily Mail* and the *Daily News*.

On another occasion, when a Liberal Cabinet Minister commented that the women's suffrage movement had not generated the kind of popular uprising associated with previous pressure groups, the suffragettes responded with a day of unprecedented destruction. On 1 March 1912, *The Times* reported that groups of fashionably dressed women smashed windows in the Strand, in Cockspur Street, in the Haymarket, and Piccadilly, in Coventry Street, in Regent Street, in part of Oxford Street and in Bond Street. Apparently, the attack was made simultaneously in the different streets, and in spite of the amount of damage done the whole disturbance was confined to a comparatively short period.

d) Arson Attacks

Arson attacks, like window breaking, were initially advanced by individuals acting on their own initiative and only later became official WSPU policy. Emily Davison's destruction of a pillar-box in December 1911 shifted militancy on to a new level – a level given the seal of approval by Emmeline Pankhurst, who said at the Albert Hall in October 1912:

1 Those of you who can express your militancy by facing Party mobs at Cabinet Ministers' meetings when you remind them of their falseness to principle – do so. Those of you who can express your militancy by join-ing us in our anti-Government by-election policy – do so. Those of you
5 who can break windows – break them. Those of you who can still fur-ther attack the secret idol of property so as to make the Government realise that property is as greatly endangered by Women Suffrage as it was by the Chartists of old – do so. And my last word to the Government: I incite this meeting to rebellion.

Although there were a few sporadic arson attacks before 1913 the par-tial destruction of Lloyd George's country house in Surrey that year marked a watershed in suffragette violence. 'We have tried blowing him up to wake his conscience,' said Emmeline Pankhurst. Many of the arson attacks were, like window-smashing, a response to particular political events. At least four of the major acts of arson committed in March 1914 were precipitated by the arrests of Emmeline Pankhurst. In Ireland, violent action, such as destroying the windows of English-owned buildings like Dublin Castle, was almost always in response to the failure of a women's suffrage amendment in England. The arson campaign was widespread throughout Britain as you can see from 'A Year's Record' on page 72.

e) Other Damaging Behaviour

Suffragettes tried to destroy valuable works of art as a protest against the higher value placed on property than on people. The most famous case centred on Mary Richardson, who walked into the National Gallery and attacked the painting of Venus by Velasquez with an axe. Mary Richardson, later known as 'Slasher Mary', wanted to draw a par-allel between the public's indifference to Emmeline Pankhurst's health and their respect for a valuable object. She said that 'You can get another picture, but you cannot get a life, as they are killing Mrs Pankhurst.'[9] (Emmeline Pankhurst was very weak at this time due to constant imprisonment and hunger-striking.) Other suffragettes used similar tactics. In the same year, a woman spoiled a painting by Romney that hung in the Birmingham Art Gallery, while another tried to mutilate the picture of the King in the Royal Scottish Academy. The WSPU cut telegraph wires, wrecked plants in Kew Greenhouse and burnt messages with acid into golf courses saying 'No Votes, No Golf'. Yet, perhaps the greatest damage the suffragettes did was to themselves. The best-known and the most tragic incident involved Emily Davison at the 1913 Derby when she jumped out in front of the king's horse and died as a result of the injuries she sustained. She was not the only one to die in the suffrage cause: Ellen Pitfield died of incurable injuries received on Black Friday 1910 (see pages 87–8). Others, including Lady Constance Lytton who suffered a stroke in

258   **THE SUFFRAGETTE**   December 26, 1913.

A YEAR'S RECORD.

The following are the more serious attacks on property which have been attributed to Suffragettes during the year 1913.

January 13.—Estimate that women have broken glass worth from £4,000 to £5,000.

January 28.—Women sentenced for damaging Windsor Castle. Fifty women arrested for window-smashing in West End of London.

January 30.—Windows of Lambeth Palace broken.

February 3.—Case smashed in jewel-room at Tower of London.

February 8.—Hundreds of orchids destroyed at Kew Gardens.

February 12.—Kiosk burnt in Regent's Park : damage £400.

February 16.—Wholesale raid on golf links, many greens being damaged.

February 17.—Great Central Railway carriage fired at Harrow.

February 19.—House building for Mr. Lloyd George blown up at Walton Heath.

March 10.—Saunderton and Croxley Green stations destroyed by fire.

March 11.—Revolver shots and vitriol thrown at Nottingham Suffragette meeting.

March 16.—£2,000 house burnt at Cheam.

March 20.—Lady White's house, Staines, burnt down; £3,000 damage.

March 24.—House set on fire at Beckenham.

March 27.—House fired at Hampstead : petrol explosion.

April 2.—Church fired at Hampstead Garden Suburb.

April 3.—Four houses fired at Hampstead Garden Suburb.

April 4.—Mansion near Chorley Wood destroyed by fire; bomb explosion at Oxted Station; empty train wrecked by bomb explosion at Devonport; famous pictures damaged at Manchester.

April 5.—Ayr racecourse stand burnt : £3,000 damage; attempt to destroy Kelso racecourse grand stand.

April 6.—House fired at Potter's Bar; mansion destroyed at Norwich.

April 8.—Plot to destroy Crystal Palace stands before the Football Cup tie.

April 8.—Explosion in grounds of Dudley Castle; bomb found in heavily-laden Kingston train at Queen's Road, Battersea.

April 11.—Tunbridge Wells cricket pavilion destroyed.

April 12.—Council schools, Gateshead, set on fire.

April 15.—Mansion fired at St. Leonard's : damage £9,000—Home Office order prohibits Suffragette meetings.

April 19.—Attempt to wreck Smeaton's famous Eddystone Lighthouse on Plymouth Hoe.

April 20.—Attempt to blow up offices of "York Herald," York, with a bomb.

April 23.—Attempt to burn Minster Church, Isle of Thanet.

April 24.—Bomb exploded at County Council offices, Newcastle.

April 26.—Railway carriage destroyed by fire at Teddington.

April 30.—Boathouse burned at Hampton Court : £3,500 damage; Suffragettes' headquarters seized by police, five leaders arrested.

May 1.—Buildings burned at Hendon.

May 3.—Amazing Suffragette plots disclosed at Bow Street.

May 6.—Woman Suffrage Bill defeated in Commons; St. Catherine's Church, Hatcham, burned down.

May 7.—Bomb found in St. Paul's Cathedral; two bungalows damaged near Bexhill; bowling-green chálet, Bishop's Park, Fulham, destroyed.

May 9.—Oakley, near Barrow, fired.

May 10.—Farringdon Hall, Dundee, destroyed : damage £10,000; private house, Beckenham, fired.

May 12.—Boathouse on the Trent destroyed : damage nearly £2,000.

May 13.—Private house, Hendon, badly destroyed.

May 14.—Private house Folkestone, fired : damage from £700 to £1,000; Penn Church damaged.

May 15.—St. Anne's Church, Eastbourne, damaged.

May 18.—Parish Rooms, St. Anne's, Eastbourne, damaged by fire; private house, Cambridge, destroyed by fire : damage between £700 to £1,000; buildings belonging to University, Cambridge, damaged.

May 21.—Bomb explosion, Blackford Observatory, Edinburgh : serious damage.

May 22.—Trinity Wesleyan Church, Stamford, burned; stables, Stamford Hotel, damaged.

May 23.—South Bromley Station damaged by fire.

May 28.—Good's Yard, G.C. Railway Station, Nottingham, timber stacks destroyed.

May 31.—Shields Road Station, Glasgow, damaged.

June 3.—Rough's boathouse, Oxford, destroyed : damage £3,000; Westwood Manor, Trowbridge, destroyed by fire : damage £15,000.

June 7.—North Middlesex Cricket Club pavilion destroyed by fire : business premises at Bradford destroyed : damage £80,000.

June 8.—Boathouse, Hollow Pond, Whipp's Cross, destroyed.

June 11.—Private house, East Lothian, destroyed : damage £7,000.

June 12.—Assembly Rooms and Pier Hotel, Withernsea, destroyed.

June 15.—Eden Park Station damaged; three further outbreaks in Bradford.

June 18.—Rowley Regis Church, near Dudley, destroyed : damage £6,000.

June 19.—Private house, Olton, destroyed.

June 21.—Gatty Marine Laboratory, St. Andrew's University, partially destroyed.

June 25.—Haslewell Railway Station damaged.

June 30.—Ballikinian Castle, Stirlingshire, destroyed : damage £70,000; Lencross Railway Station destroyed : damage £2,000.

July 4.—Private house, South Coldfiels, destroyed : damage £4,000.

July 8.—Sir W. Lever's bungalow destroyed.

July 21.—Private house, Perry Bar, damaged.

August 4.—Private house, Woldingham, damaged.

August 5.—Holiday House, Lyton, destroyed : damage £10,000; motor car burned.

August 8.—School, Sutton-in-Ashfield, damaged; private house, Finchley : damage £500; hayricks fired, Abergavenny : damage £50.

August 13.—Lazey Glen Pavilion, Isle of Man, destroyed : damage £5,000.

August 14.—Carnarvon School House damaged.

August 15.—Haystacks burned near Liverpool : damage £350; Willesden Park pavilion destroyed : damage £250.

August 16.—Private house, Bangor, damaged.

August 19.—Bedford Timber Yard : damage £300.

August 22.—Private house, Edinburgh : damage £500; Fettes College, Edinburgh, damaged.

August 23.—Haystacks burned Littlemore, Burnham Beeches, and Maltby : damage about £300; motor cars burned at Hunsworth, Birmingham.

September 1.—Bomb found in Cheltenham Town Hall; house fired at Newcastle; school fired at Oldbury; International Correspondence Schools fired at Finchley.

September 5.—Fire at Dulwich College : damage £300.

September 11.—Stanstead House, Seaton, fired : damage £500.

September 13.—Kenton Station gutted : damage £1,000.

September 16.—Wheat rick destroyed at Berkhampstead; Penshurst Place burnt.

September 19.—House fired at Finchley; house fired at Liverpool.

September 23.—Seafield House, Derby, completely gutted : damage £80,000.

September 22.—Withernsea Town Hall gutted; The Cedars, Waltham Cross, destroyed by fire; fire at Warren Hill, Loughton.

September 27.—Fire at timber yards, Yarmouth : damage £40,000.

September 28.—Fire at Frensham Hall, Farnham; Football Ground stand at Plumstead destroyed by fire : damage £1,000; hayricks fired near Oldbury : damage £200.

October 2.—Hayricks and farm fired at Willesden.

October 4.—The Elms, Hampton-on-Thames burnt out : damage £3,000.

October 7.—Two houses fired at Bedford.

October 10.—Yarmouth Pier fired.

October 12.—Wrighley Head Mill, Failsworth, fired.

October 19.—Red House, Loughborough, fired.

October 23.—Bristol Line Athletic Ground destroyed by fire : damage £2,200.

October 22.—Two stations in Birmingham fired.

October 26.—Brooklands, Farnham Royal, destroyed by fire.

October 28.—Shirley Manor, Wyke, completely destroyed by fire : damage £5,000; Mill House, Bramshill, destroyed by fire; Station fired at Oldbury.

November 2.—Streatham Station fired.

November 8.—Stockton Grand Stand fired.

November 11.—Bomb explosion in Cactus House, Alexandra Park, Manchester : damage to glass alone £200; Begbrook, Bristol, fired : damage £3,000; Bowling Green Club pavilion at Catford burned to ground : damage £1,500.

November 15.—Bomb found in Palm House, Sefton Park, Liverpool.

November 16.—The Priory, Sandown Park, Liverpool, fired : three floors and roof destroyed.

November 17.—Newton Road Station, Birmingham, fired.

November 20.—Mill at Ashton-under-Lyne fired : damage £200; fire at timber yard, Oxford : damage £3,000.

November 22.—Football Stand, Blackburn, fired.

November 23.—Bristol boathouse burned : damage £300.

November 24.—Castle Bromwich Station fired.

November 27.—Caerleon Training College, Newport, fired : damage £40,000.

November 24.—Hurristfield, hayricks burned : damage £2,000.

December 5.—Kelly House, Wemyss Bay, fired : damage £60,000.

December 6.—Rusholme Exhibition, Manchester, fired : damage £12,000; Liverpool Exhibition fired.

December 13.—Scottish mansion (Ardgare) fired : damage £10,000.

December 15.—Devonport timber yards fired, more than £2,000 damage; Bristol mansion fired.

December 16.—Liverpool church fired.

December 18.—Explosion at Holloway Prison.

MRS. PANKHURST'S LICENCE.
Readers are asked to note that Mrs. Pankhurst's last licence is on sale for the highest bidder.

A year's record of suffragette activity.

1912, were physically weakened as a result of their treatment in prison, hunger strikes and so on and many died at an early age.

These particular law-breaking activities were well orchestrated and more reminiscent of guerrilla warfare than traditional forms of political protest. In Scotland, for example, pillar-box attacks were organised with great precision. Activists would meet at a pre-arranged time and place. They would be handed bottles of acid, which had usually been obtained by sympathetic chemist members, and told exactly when to drop them into pillar-boxes for the greatest effect. While doing this kind of work suffragettes tried to remain anonymous: one activist always dressed as a domestic servant, with black dress and white muslin apron, to avoid suspicion. To ensure secrecy, all messages were written in code. At first the code word ANNOUNCEMENT was used until the secret was discovered by the press and the more impenetrable PORTUGUESE EAST AFRICA replaced it.

f) Hunger Striking

By engaging in illegal activities, the suffragettes were liable to arrest and imprisonment; once imprisoned, large numbers went on hunger strike to protest that their detention was unfair – and to gain publicity. As with the first window-smashers and the first arsonists, the first hunger-striker, Marion Wallace-Dunlop, conceived of the idea independently when imprisoned for stencilling a quotation from the Bill of Rights on a wall in the House of Commons. This action soon became official WSPU policy especially when it was realised that hunger-strikers were released from prison when their health was seen to be in danger.

The WSPU used the experiences of hunger-strikers to gain widespread sympathy. Stories regularly appeared in *Votes for Women* about the brutal way in which women were treated. The paper often drew attention to the class differences within prison by informing readers that when working-class women were forcibly fed they were not given any medical aid or examined to see if they were fit. Selina Martin, a working-class woman arrested in Liverpool, was kept in chains and frog-marched to her cell. In contrast, upper- and middle-class women were given preferential treatment and shown greater consideration. These discrepancies prompted Lady Constance Lytton, in 1911, to disguise herself as a working-class woman called Jane Wharton. Quite deliberately, she committed a criminal act, was arrested, convicted and sent to prison. As Lady Constance Lytton, she had always been medically examined and found unfit to be force-fed. As Jane Wharton she received no such care and was brutally force-fed seven times. This case attracted much publicity and enabled the WSPU to draw attention to the status differences that existed both in prison and the wider society and that the female vote might help to eliminate.

It is often assumed that this type of behaviour was orchestrated by an iconoclastic WSPU leadership that marshalled an obedient membership and directed it to commit crimes. Militancy, however, often began at a local level with a few ardent activists and was only adopted as WSPU policy when it had received overwhelming support from the membership. As Sandra Holton has pointed out, window smashing, arson, letter burning and hunger striking were all initiated by rank and file members. Indeed, there is evidence to suggest, that rather than encourage impetuous behaviour, the WSPU leadership tried to restrain the enthusiasms of its rank and file from ever-increasing violent tactics. When a Young Hot Bloods (YHB) group was formed, Emmeline Pankhurst was scrupulous in not encouraging illegal activities and often froze in disapproval when the young women members announced that they were willing to be arrested.

4 Conclusion

KEY ISSUE was violence self-defeating?

In many ways it is disappointing to see how often the suffragists and the suffragettes have continued to be written about as separate groups: on the one side, the law-abiding constitutionalist organisations, such as the NUWSS, who advocated peaceful persuasion; on the other side, the ungovernable WSPU who preferred destruction to reason. It is important to remember that the suffrage movement was one story with several subplots rather than a collection of totally different sagas. After all, the suffrage organisations shared a common goal – votes for women – and only differed on the ways to achieve it. Perhaps it is only historians, desperate to tidy up the past and impose an order on a rather chaotic movement, who need to categorise the suffrage movement in such a linear way.

The destructive methods of the WSPU have been the subject of much historical research. In 1860, when this story begins, only peaceful methods were used, whereas by 1914 suffragette violence was at its height. And it is this turn towards violence that has tended to dominate the history texts. However, the WSPU did not break with the suffragist past but built upon it; violent measures did not replace constitutional ones so much as supplement them. Throughout this whole period both the suffragists and suffragettes continued to use the traditional forms of protest such as petitioning Parliament, lobbying MPs and demonstrating. Furthermore, both the suffragists and the suffragettes often tried to end the impasse between themselves and the Liberal Government by supporting the two Conciliation Bills put forward in the House of Commons to enfranchise women. On these occasions all the suffrage organisations co-operated with each

Conciliation Committee that proposed the Bill. They lobbied MPs, sent speakers to various organisations and directed local constituency groups to put pressure on their MPs to vote for each Bill. And while negotiations continued the WSPU leadership called a truce. The Conciliation Bills, as we know, failed to become law. The defeat of each added to the injustice felt within the suffrage groups. Many NUWSS women resigned from the Liberal Party. The WSPU, for its part, reverted to its strategy of violence.

Nevertheless, there is little doubt that the NUWSS leaders grew irritated by the increasingly destructive tactics of the WSPU. Over the years, they had tried to prove that they (and, by association, women in general) were calm, sensible and rational beings. Accordingly they put forward measured arguments and used democratic methods to get their message across. It was feared that the use of violence discredited the suffrage movement and undermined suffragist efforts to be seen as mature adults who could be trusted with the vote. However, the NUWSS leaders were reluctant to criticise the WSPU openly and publicly in case this exacerbated the Government's obstinacy.

Was the violence of the suffragettes self-defeating? It is sometimes argued that it lost the WSPU the sympathy and support of the country at large and provided the Liberal Government with the perfect excuse to deny women the vote. Not surprisingly, the WSPU leaders denied the accusation that violence was counter-productive. On the contrary – to believe that militancy damaged the suffrage cause was to be ignorant of all the lessons taught by history. To their minds, peaceful tactics were ineffective as they failed to bring about any change in the law. The WSPU found that they had run out of patience and now hoped to force the government into conceding votes for women by a sustained campaign of violence. Nevertheless, the violence that the suffragettes used was restrained and circumscribed by their ideological beliefs about the sanctity of life. Although they were prepared to sacrifice their own lives in the pursuit of votes for women, the suffragettes generally confined themselves to attacks on property rather than people. Certainly, up until 1914, when the WSPU ceased its campaigning, Cabinet Ministers and others were rarely in any personal danger because Emmeline Pankhurst proclaimed that the WSPU did not wish to harm people, only property. However, it is tempting to speculate whether this belief in the sacredness of human life would have lasted if war had not broken out as, after all, the suffragettes had already begun to throw slates and other missiles at government ministers.

References

1 *Feminism and Democracy*, Sandra Holton (Cambridge University Press, 1986).
2 *Suffrage and the Pankhursts*, Jane Marcus (ed) (Routledge and Kegan Paul, 1987) p. 9.

3 Leaflet written by Christabel Pankhurst circa 1912.
4 *The Suffragette*, 12 December 1913.
5 *The Strange Death of Liberal England*, George Dangerfield (Perigree Books, 1980) p. 154.
6 'The Act of Militancy' by Brian Harrison (ed.), in *Peaceable Kingdom: Stability and Change in Modern Britain* (Clarendon Press, 1982).
7 *The Reformers' Year Book 1907*, TD Benson (Suffrage Collection, Museum of London).
8 *'A Guid Cause': The Woman's Suffrage Movement in Scotland*, L Leneman (Aberdeen University Press, 1991).
9 *The Times*, 11 March 1914.

Summary Diagram
The Suffrage Campaigns

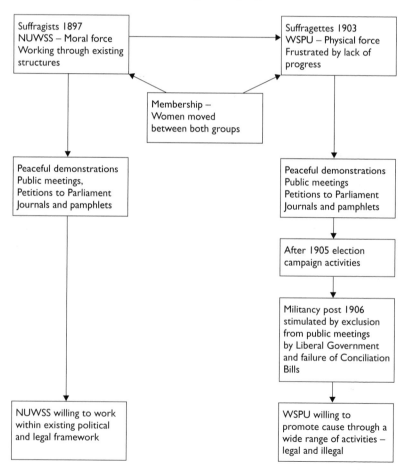

Working on Chapter 4

This chapter relates to the growing radicalism of the suffrage movement and the emerging tensions between the WSPU and the NUWSS. The failure of the campaign to extend the right for women to vote led to increasing discontent amongst those engaged in the struggle. Write notes to explain how this failure led to divisions within the women's suffrage movement, militant and non-militant, suffragettes and suffragists. To strengthen your understanding of the divisions, construct a table listing the various methods used by each group and evaluate the effectiveness of each method. When reading this Chapter keep the following questions in mind:

- What pressures drove the suffragettes to become more militant?
- To what extent did government policies drive this militancy?
- Was the policy stance of the Liberal and Tory governments justified?

Answering structured questions and essay questions on Chapter 4

It is important, when you are presented with an essay question, that you recognise the type of question that is set. There are three main types of question – analytical, evaluative or judgemental questions. A question that starts with 'What were', 'Describe', 'In what ways', or 'Account for' will expect you to make decisions about what material best fits the question. You also need to display chronological awareness, as well as organisation skills, balance within a well-constructed answer, and the prioritisation of relevant material. A question that starts with 'Why', will expect you to set out reasons, in order of importance bearing in mind how complex it is to explain historical events. The use of phrases and words such as 'To what extent', 'How far', 'Assess', 'Discuss', or 'Comment' will require you to analyse and evaluate the evidence, to reach a decision or judgement, based on your argument. If a quotation is provided that offers a particular view you can accept or reject this view based on the evidence you choose to use. Essay questions relating to this chapter are most likely to deal with the perceived divisions within the women's suffrage movement and the reasons for them.

In this chapter the suffrage campaign is characterised by the emergence of two distinct organisations committed to the extension of the franchise but choosing to go about this in different ways: militant actions and the politics of confrontation, on the one hand, and non-militant actions and the politics of persuasion, on the other. Generally, debate among historians has centred on the extent of difference between the Women's Social and Political Union and the National Union of Women's Suffrage Societies.

Look at the following essay examples:

1 How valid is the view that the NUWSS was hostile towards the WSPU because its members used violent methods in the years 1903–13?
2 To what extent could it be argued that the violent methods of the WSPU compared to the constitutional methods of the NUWSS hindered rather than helped the cause of female suffrage by 1914?
3 Do you agree with the view that the militancy of the WSPU was the main reason why women had not been given the right to vote by 1914?
4 Why did the WSPU turn from the politics of persuasion to the politics of confrontation and militant tactics in the struggle for the vote?

When making a plan to answer Question 2, draw up a list of methods used by the WSPU and the NUWSS. Opposite each method note the extent to which it hindered or furthered the progress of female suffrage. Then consider other reasons for the failure of female suffrage. For example, the Irish Question and the amount of Parliamentary time spent on this in comparison to the amount of time spent on the rights of women and the vote. In this question you will need to discuss fully the various reasons for the different methods and the implications of these for the furtherance of the women's suffrage movement. An effective conclusion to this question will require you to decide which of the reasons was of most importance and why.

The following are two examples of structured questions relating to this chapter. The format with a structured question will usually involve two parts. The first part will as a rule require you to describe or explain why something occurred – it will test how you use your knowledge to make judgements. In the second part you will be asked to evaluate a range of factors. For both parts you will need to be selective in the material you use and you may need to come to some sort of judgement. Consider the following examples:

1 **a)** Describe the methods used by the suffragettes/gists to gain the right to vote in the years 1906–14. (*8 marks*)
   b) Do you agree with the view that the militancy of the WSPU hindered rather than helped the cause of female suffrage by 1914? (*12 marks*)
2 **a)** Why did the NUWSS redirect their allegiance to the Labour Party from 1912 onwards? (*8 marks*)
   b) How successful were the Liberal government in dealing with the militancy of the WSPU in the years 1906–14? (*12 marks*)

5 Men and Votes for Women

POINTS TO CONSIDER

The main issue to consider when reading this chapter is the extent to which men supported or opposed women's suffrage. By the end of the chapter you should be familiar with the attitudes of the political parties to women's suffrage and begin to understand why the Liberal Party did not enfranchise women. Outside formal political circles, men tended to react differently to the notion of votes for women. This chapter should help you understand the diversity of male responses to this complex political issue.

KEY DATES

1832 Henry Hunt introduced first petition in support of women's suffrage to Parliament

1866 J S Mill presented women's suffrage to Parliament

1867 Mill's amendment to include women in the Second Reform Bill defeated

1906 Liberal landslide election victory

1909 Second reading of electoral Reform Bill, which included votes for women; suffragettes banned from Liberal meetings; first forcible feeding

1910 Conciliation Bill passed but effectively shelved; Black Friday

1911 Failure of Second Conciliation Bill

1912 Third Conciliation Bill failed its second reading; Electoral Fighting Fund established

1913 Amendment to franchise bill ruled out of order by Speaker; Cat and Mouse Act passed.

It is tempting to classify the struggle for votes for women as a battle of the sexes; but, in fact, the lines of engagement between women and men were not so clearly drawn. At first, it appears that men generally disagreed with votes for women – certainly no government was prepared to enfranchise them. Indeed, mention of female suffrage within Parliament was often greeted by ribald laughter and antagonistic speeches. However, men, just like women, were not a homogeneous group but were made up of individuals from diverse economic and social backgrounds who held a variety of political views. As a consequence, there emerged several different male perspectives on women's suffrage, and it is worth exploring the extent to which men either opposed or championed the suffrage movement. Despite setbacks, by 1914 suffrage had certainly become the foremost political question for women and was firmly on the national agenda of male politics.

1 The Political Parties

KEY ISSUE What were the similarities and differences between the political parties on the issue of votes for women?

Even though suffrage eventually became headline news, no party before 1918 was prepared to adopt women's suffrage as their official policy. As a result, all the suffrage bills in parliament were put forward by sympathetic MPs as private members' bills, which had little chance of success since they did not have majority party backing. Between 1860 and 1914 no bill for women's suffrage ever got beyond its second reading. (Each bill has to go through three readings in Parliament before it becomes law.) When women's suffrage was first debated, in 1867, there were 71 votes for and 123 against, but most abstained from voting. Practically every year for the following 40 years a women's franchise bill was introduced – and failed. Not only did each Bill fail but the debates surrounding them were usually characterised by facetious or hostile speeches from Honourable Members. In 1905 MPs debated for hours, with mock seriousness, a measure to compel carts on the road to carry rear lights – to avoid giving time to a bill on women's suffrage. Eventually, in 1910, in an attempt to break the party deadlock, a group of MPs from all sides of the House of Commons formed a Conciliation Committee, which consisted of 25 Liberals, 17 Conservative, six Labour and six Irish Nationalists, to marshal support across party lines. This Committee continued the tradition of sponsoring private members' bills but, although the MPs who presented each bill gained support from a few sympathisers, they faced greater opposition.

Why was women's suffrage so unsuccessful in gaining wholesale party approval? It has been argued that Conservatives disliked any extension of democracy, whereas the Liberals, fearful of the property-based qualification for the vote, were convinced that women would support the Conservatives. There was certainly a historical precedent for this fear because, when the Liberals passed the Third Reform Bill in 1884, many of the agricultural labourers who were enfranchised voted Conservative. Labour, of course, much preferred universal franchise to what was perceived to be a middle-class female vote. However, such a clear-cut party interpretation underestimates the variety of opinions that existed within the parties concerned.

a) The Conservative Party

Votes for women found favour within some sections of the Conservative Party. Women's suffrage resolutions were passed at Conservative Party Annual Conferences in England on at least three occasions and by Scottish Annual Conferences more regularly. Most of the Conservative Party leadership seemed well disposed towards votes for women: Prime Ministers Disraeli, Salisbury and Balfour, for example, all spoke in support. In 1866 Disraeli stated that 'I do not see ... on what reasons ... she has not a right to vote';[1] in 1888, Lord Salisbury believed 'that the day is not far distant when women will also bear their share in voting for members of Parliament and in determining the policy of the country';[2] and in 1892 Balfour pointed out the contradiction in giving 'a vote to a man who contributes nothing to taxation but what he pays on his beer, while you refuse enfranchisement to a woman whatever her contribution to the state may be'.[3] Some Conservative MPs even promoted private members' bills within the House of Commons and worked hard for the all-party Conciliation Committee established in 1910.

However, as Rover points out, there was no evidence of any great commitment by the Conservative leaders to implement women's suffrage when they were in office. When John Stuart Mill proposed a woman's suffrage amendment to the 1867 Reform Bill, Disraeli (who was prepared to take a 'leap in the dark' to extend the franchise to working-class men) offered no help towards its safe passage. Similarly Lord Salisbury did little to further the cause of women's suffrage and even voted against a second reading of a women's suffrage Bill in 1891. His nephew, Arthur Balfour, considered sympathetic to women's suffrage, again did little. When Balfour was succeeded as Conservative leader by Bonar Law the suffrage movement fared no better: in 1913 Bonar Law declined to support an amendment to a franchise reform bill that would have given women the vote.

Nonetheless, as Pugh points out, the fact that Conservative leaders sympathised with the principle of votes for women made it easier, and politically respectable, for MPs to introduce their own Private Members' bills in favour of women's suffrage. Several women's suffrage bills were put forward by Conservative MPs as private members' bills: in 1874 by Forsyth, in 1888 by Dimsdale, in 1892 by Rollit, in 1895 by Madona, in 1896 by Begg, in 1903 by Denny and in 1912 by Agg-Gardner. These bills may not have succeeded but they kept votes for women in the Parliamentary, and the public, eye. During the 1870s a number of Conservatives began to realise that there might be some party advantage if the vote was granted to propertied women. 'It was not so much a question of the rights of women, as of the rights of property' said one MP.[4] From the 1890s until 1908 there was a significant shift among Conservatives with the majority of their MPs supporting the women's suffrage bills put forward. By the Edwardian period, most MPs recognised the inevitability of votes for women, even though they disapproved of suffragette methods. Nonetheless, women's suffrage never became party policy.

The predominantly Conservative House of Lords was generally opposed to women's suffrage but there were notable exceptions. Lord Lytton, Constance Lytton's brother and President of the Men's

League for Women's Suffrage, was in favour of Votes for Women and systematically promoted the cause within the House of Lords. However, most shared the views of Lord Curzon, who was antagonistic towards female suffrage. As Vice President of the Men's League for Opposing Women's Suffrage, he actively campaigned against votes for women, believing that militancy resulted from the mental instability of women. Many Conservatives agreed with Curzon's sentiments and were convinced that madness would ensue once women were enfranchised. Even so, the number of Conservatives who disagreed with votes for women decreased year by year.

b) The Liberal Party

In the early years, the campaign to enfranchise women was undoubtedly endorsed by the Liberals but the party soon became split over the question. In the 1860s the suffrage campaign had been launched by leading Liberal intellectuals who saw women's enfranchisement as a basic human right. However, the more traditional wing of the Liberal party did not hold these views, sharing the conventional opinion that women's role was in the home not the House of Commons.

As a general rule, Liberal prime ministers refused to support votes for women. In the nineteenth century Prime Minister Gladstone was ambivalent over the idea of women's suffrage, sometimes raising women's hopes by speaking in favour of female suffrage yet later letting it be known that he, and any governments he formed, would oppose any amendment to enfranchise women. Indeed, when he was in office, Gladstone opposed a women's suffrage amendment to the 1884 Reform Bill on the grounds that it might endanger its successful passing. In a letter to an MP in 1892 he stated that 'The fear I have is, we should invite her unwittingly to trespass upon the delicacy, the purity, the refinement, the elevation of her own nature'.[5] In the early twentieth century Campbell-Bannerman privately expressed approval of votes for women but publicly blocked its progress in the House of Commons. Historians have pinpointed the entrenched position of Asquith, prime minister at the height of suffragette militancy, who obstructed every move towards accepting votes for women and persistently refused to see women's suffrage deputations. Asquith, although married to a very shrewd political operator, was unchanging in his implacable opposition to votes for women. In his first major speech on suffrage in 1892 he gave four main reasons why he was against women's suffrage: the vast majority of women did not want the vote; women were not fit for the franchise; women operated best by personal influence; and (anyway) it would upset the natural order of things. Asquith believed that woman's place was in the home rather than in what he termed the 'dust and turmoil' of political life. Indeed it is commonly accepted that it was Asquith more than any other person who prevented the Liberal Party from becoming the party to enfranchise women.

Women's suffrage drew support from leading Liberal MPs but this support, as with the Conservatives, was sometimes faint-hearted. Both Lloyd George and Winston Churchill advocated women's suffrage at various meetings but opposed the first Conciliation Bill of 1910 (see page 80) because it offered too limited a franchise. And, in 1912, when a further Conciliation Bill was being debated in Parliament, both Lloyd George and Churchill were associated with a rumour that Asquith would resign if the Bill were passed. However, when he was Prime Minister, Lloyd George was responsible for the safe passage of the 1918 Reform Bill, which enfranchised women over the age of 30.

Despite the antagonism from prime ministers and the feeble support of many leading Liberals, a number of individuals gave generously of their time, money and energies to promote votes for women. In the nineteenth century the MPs Jacob Bright, Charles Dilke, Henry Fawcett, James Stansfeld and John Stuart Mill and the barrister Richard Pankhurst were just some of many men who supported votes for women, often at the expense of other commitments. Between 1867 and 1886, when there were 15 women's suffrage resolutions, the Liberals accounted for more than two-thirds of the Yes votes. In the twentieth century, William Barton (Oldham) and Henry Harben (Barnstaple) both gave up their seats because of the Liberal Government's reluctance to enfranchise women, whereas the leading Liberal Sir John Simon accepted the Vice Presidency of the Manchester Men's League (for women's suffrage), which could have damaged his parliamentary career. Frederick Pethick-Lawrence put his life and finance at risk, was forcibly fed in prison and was declared bankrupt when his fortune was sequestered as a result of his suffragette activities. And there is little doubt that the 25 Liberal MPs who worked hard for the Conciliation Committee were deeply committed to female suffrage.

In the 1880s women's suffrage was overtaken by the debate over Home Rule within the Liberal Party and received a blow when the party split in 1886 into the Gladstonian Liberals and the Liberal Unionists. The leaders of the newly formed Liberal Unionists tended to be antagonistic to women's suffrage whereas the Gladstone wing was more sympathetic. Gradually, as New Liberalism emerged from the Gladstonian section, support for women's suffrage increased and votes for women once more became a Liberal issue.

c) The Labour Party

The Labour Party, which emerged from the Labour Representation Committee, was founded in 1906 – the same year that the Liberals swept to power. Initially, the Labour Party's support for votes for women was somewhat muted as the Party was split over whether to champion women's suffrage at the expense of universal suffrage. Even in 1900, roughly 60 per cent of working-class men were excluded from the franchise as the right to vote was still based upon the ownership or occupation of property. Because women demanded the vote on the same terms as men, many Labour Party members (who saw universal suffrage as being of greater importance) were unsympathetic towards such an elitist measure. In addition they feared that a limited franchise would be detrimental to the Labour Party as it would increase the political power of the propertied class and reinforce the class composition of the voting population. Indeed it became a socialist imperative to call for adult suffrage rather than female suffrage. By 1907, as June Hanham points out, 'it had become more difficult to combine labour and suffrage politics' particularly when the disruptive tactics of the suffragettes at by-elections strained any residual loyalties the labour movement held about votes for women.[6]

A future leader of the Labour Party, Ramsey MacDonald, was certainly equivocal in his support of women's suffrage. Although MacDonald sympathised with women's suffrage and believed that it was a vital part of a socialist programme, he was overtly critical of the methods of the suffragettes:

> 1 I have no objection to revolution, if it is necessary, but I have the very strongest objection to childishness masquerading as revolution, and all I can say of these window-breaking expeditions is that they are simply silly and provocative. I wish the working women of the country who really
> 5 care for the vote ... would come to London and tell these pettifogging middle-class damsels who are going out with little hammers in their muffs that if they do not go home they will get their heads broken.[7]

In contrast, three key Labour MPs, Keir Hardie, George Lansbury and Philip Snowden, took a more pragmatic view of reform. They argued that it was crucial to fight one step at a time and preferred to campaign for votes for women, which they claimed would affect the majority of working-class widows and spinsters, rather than wait for universal suffrage. Keir Hardie (a close friend of the Pankhursts, and one-time lover of Sylvia) worked hard for women's suffrage both in and outside Parliament. Although he was often ridiculed in the House of Commons Keir Hardie's commitment never wavered. According to Sylvia Pankhurst, he collected funds, wrote leaflets, taught the suffragettes Parliamentary procedure, introduced them to influential people, visited them in prison and even condoned their violent tactics. Similarly Philip Snowden, MP and vice-president of the Men's League for Women's Suffrage, promoted WSPU policies at least until 1912 when suffragette militancy reached a new height. George Lansbury, MP for Bromley and Bow, also dedicated much of his political life to women's suffrage. He condoned suffragette violence, justifying it as a response to Government duplicity. On one occasion he rushed across the House of Commons floor, shook his fist at Asquith and shouted 'You'll go down to history as the man who tortured innocent women' in objection to the force-feeding of suffragettes. Moreover, Lansbury demanded that all Labour MPs vote against all Liberal Government proposals, even when they benefited the working class, until women were granted the vote. In 1912 he resigned his seat and sought re-election as an independent MP in protest against the Labour Party's half-hearted commitment to women's suffrage. This was an act of great generosity – or foolishness – because Lansbury failed to get elected. The social reformer Beatrice Webb described him as having a great heart but too little intellect.

Relationships between the Labour Party as a whole and the suffrage movement changed over time. At first the links between the two were strong, especially at a local level: after all, the Manchester-based WSPU was founded to improve the lives of working-class women. Certainly, the agitation for women's suffrage was seen to be inextricably bound up with Labour politics. Many radical suffragists, not just the Pankhursts, joined the Labour Party. In 1906 the Women's Labour League was founded to provide socialist women with an organisational base from which to raise the issue of votes for women within the movement. Local Labour groups often supported women's suffrage: the Woolwich Labour Party, for example, consistently supported the aims and methods of the WSPU because they realised that even a limited extension of the franchise would give a respectable number of working-class widows and spinsters the vote. However, not all local groups supported the suffrage movement. Lewisham Borough Council for instance laughingly declined to support women's suffrage when a motion was being debated at a Council meeting. Moreover, the friendly relationship that existed between the WSPU and the Labour Party soured when the former engaged in violent behaviour and the latter refused to join George Lansbury in his opposition to the Liberal Government.

Gradually, those in favour of votes for women won the day. From 1910 onwards all Labour MPs voted in support of women's suffrage and in 1912 the NUWSS broke with their Liberal past and turned instead to the Labour Party for support. In return the NUWSS promised to raise funds to promote Labour candidates and to help organise the Labour Campaign. The Election Fighting Fund that was set up was, according to Pugh, the most important intitiative of the last 3 years of the pre-war campaign. In 1912, unsurprisingly, the Labour Party became the first major political party to include votes for women in their manifesto. Nevertheless, support for female suffrage from such a minority party (the Labour Party only had 42 MPs at the time, and even this small number was as a result of a 'secret' pact with the Liberals), did not guarantee success in Parliament.

2 The Liberal Government 1906–14

KEY ISSUES Why was the Liberal Government so unsympathetic to votes for women? How did the Liberal Government make known its position on the issue?

a) Reaction to Peaceful Campaigning

From 1906 to 1910 the Liberal Government enjoyed a large majority and therefore had the Parliamentary power to enfranchise women. Given the fact that votes for women was largely a Liberal cause it might have been expected that the Government would give women the vote. Historians have suggested that the Liberals were reluctant to do so for three main reasons. Firstly, the Prime Minister, Asquith, was hostile to votes for women. Secondly, its majority was gradually whittled down by a series of elections and from 1910 it relied on the votes from the Irish Nationalists and the Labour Party to stay in office. It was unwilling to jeopardise its term of government (the Irish Nationalists were not in favour of giving Parliamentary time to women's suffrage) for the sake of votes for women. Thirdly, the Liberals had other, more pressing, problems with which to grapple. They faced insurrection in Ireland, rebellion by the House of Lords and widespread strike action by trade unionists. It was a period George Dangerfield has characterised as 'revolutionary'. This turbulent state of affairs perhaps explains the unwillingness of a Liberal government to put time aside for a women's suffrage bill. Finally, of course, the Liberals feared that if they gave women the vote it would help the Conservatives win office. However, these suggestions can be considered excuses rather than explanations. As we have seen previously, the Liberals were ambivalent about women's suffrage and refused to promote it as party policy. Constantly, and with consummate skill, the government undermined the efforts of the advocates of women's suffrage. The following catalogue of failed bills tends to support this argument:

The Liberal Government and Votes for Women

1906	Government refused to support an amendment to a Plural Voting Bill that would have enfranchised a number of propertied women.
1907	Women's Suffrage Bill rejected.
1908	Women's Suffrage Bill passed first reading
1909	Second Reading of Women's Suffrage Bill carried but Asquith failed to give support so the Bill failed.
1910	First Conciliation Bill carried but ultimately failed because the Government refused to grant it Parliamentary time.
1911	Second Conciliation Bill carried but Asquith announced that he preferred to support manhood suffrage. A new bill could include an amendment for the enfranchisement of women.
1912	Third Conciliation Bill failed.
1913	Government Franchise Bill introduced universal male suffrage but an amendment to enfranchise women was declared unconstitutional.

Time after time, women were led to believe that votes for women were achievable only to be let down and humiliated by what they quickly perceived to be a duplicitous government. Ultimately, of course, the Liberal Government was considered by the suffragettes not just equivocal in its response to votes for women but antagonistic. The response of the Liberal Government towards women who broke the law certainly suggests that it was hostile to votes for women. There was a decided contrast between the treatment meted out to the law-breaking Ulster Unionists (who preached sedition in Belfast and smuggled guns to help a rebellion against the forthcoming partition of Ireland), and the law-breaking suffragettes. A blind eye was turned to the gun-smuggling of the Ulster rebels who remained immune from arrest and were consulted over Ireland, whereas the suffragettes were first ignored and then harassed, arrested, imprisoned, and force-fed.

When the Women's Social and Political Union (WSPU) began its illegal activities, the Liberal government reacted by denying them democratic forms of protest. In an attempt to stop potential disruption, women were forbidden to attend Liberal meetings unless they held a signed ticket. The Government refused to meet deputations or accept petitions, banned meetings in public places and censored the press in an attempt to silence the WSPU. The Commissioner of Police, directed by the Home Office, refused to allow suffragettes to hold meetings in any London parks and persuaded the management at the Albert Hall not to let it out to suffragettes. When the WSPU managed to hire a different venue, the owner of the hall was threatened with the withdrawal of his licence. The Government also prosecuted the printer who printed *The Suffragette*, periodically raided the offices and homes of the WSPU members and eventually forced Christabel Pankhurst to flee to Paris, where she directed the movement from exile.

On numerous occasions the Government acted even more harshly towards the suffragettes. As Home Secretary in charge of civil order, Winston Churchill was held responsible for the notorious police violence towards women on Friday 18 November 1910 – later termed 'Black Friday' by the suffragettes. On this day approximately 300 suffragettes marched to the House of Commons in protest at the failure of the first Conciliation Bill. When they tried to enter Parliament the police behaved with unexpected brutality. The police, instructed not to arrest the suffragettes, forced the women back, kicked them, twisted their breasts, punched their noses and thrust knees between their legs. All the 135 statements made by the suffragettes testify to the violence: 'I was seized by several policemen. One twisted my right arm behind my back with such brutal force, that I really thought he would break it ... Another policemen gave me a terrible blow in my back, which sent me whirling among the crowd',[8] said one 60-year-old woman, and 29 women testified to some form of sexual assault.

Historians offer different interpretations of this event. Rosen excuses police cruelty by suggesting that the men brought in for this day had lacked experience of handling suffragette demonstrations. In the past, he argues, they had been used to policing the rough and tough working class of the East End rather than young, genteel, middle-class women: they were at a loss to know what the correct procedure might be. In addition, women, by their very femininity, were seen to provoke police violence. 'By attempting to rush through or past police lines, these women were bringing themselves repeatedly into abrupt physical contact with the police. That the police found in the youthful femininity of many of their assailants an invitation to licence, does not seem, all in all, completely surprising'.[9] In contrast, Susan Kingsley Kent and Martha Vicinus argue that the violence directed at the suffragettes was in fact sexual abuse. The cruelty meted out by the police is seen by such historians to be a direct result of the domestic ideology of Victorian and Edwardian Britain, whereby respectable women remained in the private sphere of home while only men and prostitutes entered the public sphere of the streets. Hence, when suffragettes demonstrated outside the male Parliament they were perceived to be no better than prostitutes. Because of this, and in order to protect their public space, men were willing to permit, even encourage, 'the violation of woman's most intimate space – her body'.[10]

b) Reaction to Violent Campaigning

The Liberal Government also imprisoned suffragettes who broke the law. At first women were given 'First Division' treatment, that is, they were awarded the status of political prisoners, and so allowed to wear their own clothes and receive food parcels. After 1908, however, women were placed in the 'Second Division'. This meant they were regarded as criminals rather than political dissidents. The privileges they had once enjoyed were taken away and they were treated just like ordinary prisoners. June Purvis[11] argues that the prison authorities hoped to undermine suffragettes by making them endure ritualistic humiliation that took away their sense of self. Prisoners had to remain silent, were locked in separate cells, forced to wear prison clothes and were referred to by their prison number rather than their name. Daily life was well regulated and equally demeaning. Prisoners were woken at 5:30 a.m., ate a breakfast of tea, brown bread and butter; at 7 a.m. they had to empty the slops, scrub the cell floor and clean their tin utensils and fold their bedclothes. Baths were taken weekly and books borrowed twice a week. Each prisoner was expected to do prison work such as making night-gowns or knitting socks. At 8 p.m. the cell light was switched off. Contact with the outside world was limited – and censored. All correspondence was read by the prison authorities, which once more served to humiliate the suffragette prisoner because it invaded her privacy.

When women responded to their imprisonment by going on hunger-strike the Home Secretary, Reginald McKenna, in a debate in the House of Commons on 11 June 1914, suggested four solutions to this problem:

1 So far as I am aware these are four, and four only in number. I have had unlimited correspondence from every section of the public who have been good enough to advise me as to what I ought to do, and among them all I have not been able to discover more than four alternative
5 methods. The first, is to let them die. That is, I should say, at the present moment, the most popular, judging by the number of letters I have received. The second is to deport them. The third is to treat them as lunatic, and the fourth is to give them the franchise … I think we should not adopt any of them.

At first, hunger-strikers were released from prison but soon the government introduced force-feeding for women who consistently refused to eat. Once again, historians are divided over the significance of this course of action. Some historians justify the force-feeding of suffragettes because it saved the lives of those on hunger strike. Roger Fulford dismisses the force-feeding by the Liberal Government as a harmless procedure that had been in use for years with 'lunatics'. Early feminist historians tended to agree with these interpretations. In particular, socialist feminist historians, often antagonistic to the suffragettes, underplay the brutality of the government towards women. In stark contrast, much of the pictorial propaganda of the suffragettes represented force-feeding as oral rape. Later feminist historians subscribed to this image, arguing that the 'instrumental invasion of the body, accompanied by overpowering physical force, great suffering and humiliation was akin to it'.[12] Over 1000 women endured what Marcus calls the public violation of their bodies as they were force-fed through the nostril, the mouth and, albeit very rarely, even the rectum and vagina. Sometimes the tubes used were not sterile and had been used before which increased the sense of outrage of those who had been force-fed. On 12 August 1912, the medical journal *The Lancet*, disgusted by the practice of forcible feeding, described it as follows:

1 Prisoners were held down by force, flung on the floor, tied to chairs and iron bedsteads … while the tube was forced up the nostrils. After each feeding the nasal pain gets worse. The wardress endeavoured to make the prisoner open her mouth by sawing the edge of the cup along
5 the gums… the broken edge caused laceration and severe pain. Food into the lung of one unresisting prisoner immediately caused severe choking, vomiting … persistent coughing. She was hurriedly released next day suffering from pneumonia and pleurisy. We cannot believe that any of our colleagues will agree that this form of prison treatment is
10 justly described in Mr McKenna's words as necessary medical treatment.

Force-feeding, and the association of hunger strikers with lunatics, certainly seems to suggest that the Government was deeply hostile to suffragette prisoners. But it could equally suggest that the Liberal Government chose this method because it was alarmed at the prospect of women dying in prison. Nevertheless, the Government chose its victims with care. On the one hand, influential women like Lady Constance Lytton and Mrs Brailsford (wife of an important journalist who supported the Liberal party) were released from prison when they went on hunger strike, whereas working-class women, received quite different treatment (see page 73).

On 25 April 1913, as a result of adverse publicity, the Prisoners' Temporary Discharge for Ill-Health Act became law. This temporarily released persistent hunger-strikers from prison to give them time to recover. As soon as they were better they were required to return to prison. Not surprisingly, no woman went back to prison voluntarily. Consequently the police kept released prisoners under surveillance, arrested them and imprisoned them without trial for the same offence once they were deemed to be fit enough to serve their sentence. Would this new piece of legislation prove an effective solution to the problem of hunger striking? The suffragettes called it the 'Cat and Mouse Act'. Of course, it could be argued that the Liberal Government was merely responding in a rational way to an

PUSS-IN-BOOTS McKENNA (to his Master): "They don't seem afraid of my new mouse trap, do they?"
MARQUIS OF CARABBAS ASQUITH: "Mice are not what they used to be in the good old Constitutional days."
" *The Suffragists themselves view the Bill with mingled scorn and amusement.*"—*Evening Paper.*

Cartoon of Asquith and McKenna (Home Secretary) with suffragette 'mice',
Votes for Women, 4 April 1913.

increasing level of suffragette violence. To enfranchise women under such circumstance might well set a dangerous precedent: future protest groups could be tempted to use similar methods to achieve their goal.

3 The Alternative Establishment

> **KEY ISSUES** Which groups of men were broadly supportive of votes for women? What were the arguments of those who were antagonistic?

The male 'alternative establishment', that is the trade unions, religious groups and the press, was as divided as the political parties over the question of votes for women. Although the leadership of the majority of trade unions seemed to be indifferent to women's suffrage, a number of them supported it. Similarly, whereas the official Church was unresponsive to votes for women, some committed individual clergy campaigned vigorously for the cause. The press, depending on its political allegiances, also responded in a variety of ways. However, there is still a lot of research needed in these areas and so it is impossible to reach any definite conclusion.

a) Trade Unions

The trade union movement as a whole was divided over the question of votes for women. John Burns, a notable trade unionist, was implacably opposed to women's suffrage, whereas others agreed with it. According to Liddington and Norris, the official union response ranged from 'benign indifference to downright hostility'.[13] Although the Trades Union Congress (TUC) had passed a resolution in 1884 in favour of votes for women, little had been done to promote women's suffrage in practice. What is more, when the issue was raised 17 years later at another TUC Conference (where there were only four women delegates), it provoked a decidely hostile response. Indeed, the National Union of Miners (NUM), which controlled a large block of votes, opposed a resolution on women's suffrage at the 1912 Labour Party Conference.

However, not all the trade union movement was antagonistic as, like the Labour Party, it responded differently at individual and local levels. For example, one of the miners' leaders, Robert Smillie, advocated strike action in support of women's suffrage, and a member of the National Transport Workers' Federation was arrested and imprisoned for 2 months for breaking windows as a protest against the unjust imprisonment of suffragettes. In Glasgow dockers supported the WSPU. In Lancashire, a textile area with a history of women's active participation in the trade union movement, several weavers' unions sent petitions to Parliament and encouraged Labour MPs to introduce women's suffrage into the House of Commons. In the East End of London, Sylvia Pankhurst's East London Federation of Suffragettes (ELFS) drew support from large sections of the male working class – dockers, seamen, gas workers, labourers, firemen and post office workers – many of whom came on demonstrations and protected the ELFS members from gangs of unruly local youths. Indeed, one prize-fighter from the East End became Sylvia Pankhurst's personal bodyguard.

b) Religious Groups

Historians have virtually ignored the response of official religion to women's suffrage, even though church-going was much more central to people's lives in the nineteenth and early twentieth centuries. Despite this lack of research, it seems safe to say that religious groups responded to women's suffrage in diverse ways. The Church of England was somewhat ambivalent, whereas Nonconformists (Protestants outside the Church of England), and Quakers in particular, sometimes gave unqualified support. To date, there has been no published research on either the Roman Catholic or Judaism's response though it is known that a Canon of a Roman Catholic Church in London supported votes for women, as did the Chief Rabbi. Catholic congregations seemed less enthusiastic than their clergy, if the experience of the ELFS was common: when a group tried to pray for women's suffrage in a Roman Catholic Church in Poplar they were beaten up by the people attending.

Throughout this period the Church of England maintained a discreet silence over the question of women's suffrage and was later criticised by the suffragettes for doing so. The WSPU condemned the church for being 'shamefully and obsequiously compliant' and for being 'degraded into the position of hanger-on and lackey of the Government'.[14] The Church of England, acting through the Bishops in the House of Lords, was also censured for helping the Government to pass the Cat and Mouse Act. Indeed the Church of England was thought to disapprove more of militancy than forcible feeding, and this prompted the WSPU's blistering attack on the Church for

i   having aided and abetted the State in robbing women of the vote. The Church is thus held guilty of the subjection of women and all the vice, suffering and social degradation that result from that subjection. Whereas it is the duty of the Church to insist upon the political enfran-
5   chisement of women – not only as a political reform, but as a moral and even a religious reform – the Church has actually boycotted this great question and has condoned the torture of the women who are fighting for their liberty.[15]

Nevertheless individual clergy responded positively to women's suffrage. Significant leaders of Anglican religious thought in the early twentieth century – the Archbishop of Canterbury, the Lord Bishop of Exeter, the Lord Bishop of Hereford, the Lord Bishop of Liverpool and the Right Rev. Bishop of Edinburgh – favoured votes for women. A number of clergy, who argued that women's suffrage harmonised with essential Christian principles of equality, established a Church League for Women's Suffrage to promote the cause. The Rector of Whitburn, for example, said that the

i extension of the Suffrage to women seems to me a logical sequence of Christian principle. In the Christian society there is no superior sex, the equality of each member is recognised, the individuality of each person is sacred. St Paul asserted this when he wrote: 'in baptism there is
5 neither male nor female'. The rights of each are equal, therefore women are entitled to express their convictions and assert their individuality by voting if they choose to do so.[16]

Similarly, the Vicar at Kirkby Lonsdale believed that because Jesus Christ encouraged a certain freedom and independence in the conduct of women then it followed that Christians should support women's suffrage. Others believed women to be the moral guardians of the nation and the family who, once enfranchised, would exercise a beneficial influence on these areas. And when forcible feeding was introduced, a large number of these clergy protested against it.

The connections between suffrage and nonconformism appear much stronger. This may have been because Nonconformist women, unlike those in the Church of England, played a leading role. For example, the Labour Churches, founded in Manchester in the latter part of the nineteenth century, encouraged women to participate on equal terms and invited suffragettes like Hannah Mitchell to speak to their congregations about votes for women. Similarly, the Quakers were sympathetic to women's suffrage. Quaker women enjoyed equal rights with male Quakers, having the opportunity both to speak at religious meetings and to participate in political events. Quakers were especially motivated by a sense of moral purpose and took a leading role in many reform movements such as anti-slavery, education for women and opposition to the Contagious Diseases Acts (CDAs).

c) The Press

The press, just as religion, had been largely ignored by suffrage scholars, but there are a few general points one can make. Before the illegal activities of the WSPU provided headline-catching news, most newspapers frankly ignored the women's suffrage movement. After 1905, when Christabel Pankhurst and Annie Kenney were arrested, newspapers took more notice of suffragette activity. However, the press often reported militancy in ways that were condemnatory rather than complimentary or neutral. Once the militant campaign escalated, the response to the suffragettes grew even more hostile, with the press describing the suffragettes as mad, unladylike and misguided. *The Times*, in particular, was most unsympathetic. In 1912 it viewed the suffragettes as 'regrettable bye-products of our civilisation, out with their hammers and their bags full of stones because of dreary, empty lives and high-strung, over-excitable natures'.[17] Letters to *The Times* also suggest a deep antagonism towards women's suffrage, especially when comparisons were drawn between suffragette militancy and 'the explosive fury of epileptics'.[18] In a similar fashion the *London Standard* condemned militancy as the act of deranged lunatics and a 'form of hysteria of a highly dangerous type'.[19] Both the *Daily Mirror* and the *Illustrated London News* carried full pages of photographs of suffragettes being assaulted on Black Friday that, because of their sexually suggestive nature, were guaranteed to appeal to the prurient.

Not all newspapers were unsympathetic. At the other end of the political spectrum, *The Workman's Times* supported votes for women. Nevertheless, it shared more than a name in common with the 'official' *Times* as it too believed that women's place was in the home not the workplace.[19] The Liberal paper, the *Manchester Guardian*, the Labour *Daily Herald* and the *Daily News* all supported votes for women. Some men even published their own newspapers in support of votes for women: in 1907 J Francis began a weekly paper, *Women's Franchise*. Some local newspapers also gave qualified approval to votes for women: the *Lewisham Borough News*, for example, was sympathetic to women's suffrage but criticised the militant tactics of the WSPU.[20]

4 Male Organisations

> **KEY ISSUE** How could men make their support for the suffrage movement visible?

Men could be members of the NUWSS but were not eligible to join the WSPU – the Pankhursts believed that the suffrage struggle was a women's movement that could only be conducted by women. Thus, men founded their own organisations to support the suffragettes: the Men's League for Women's Suffrage and the Men's Federation for Women's Suffrage (this later became the Men's Political Union) were two of the most important. Others included the Men's Society for Women's Rights, the Male Electors' League for Women's Suffrage and the Liberal Men's Association for Women's Suffrage. There were also local men's organisations such as the Rebels' Social and Political Union and the East London Men's Society in the East End of London, and the Northern Men's Federation for Women's Suffrage.

Cartoon from the *Daily Mirror* on the response of museums to women visitors.

The first male-only organisation, the Men's League for Women's Suffrage, was established in 1907 and attracted men from all shades of political and religious opinion. It formed branches all over Britain: a branch was even formed as far north as Inverness. Although the League was founded by Emmeline Pethwick-Lawrence's brother-in-law and had Lord Lytton as President, it appeared to have more in common with the NUWSS and the WFL rather than the WSPU. Both Fawcett and Despard (notably not the Pankhursts) attended its first public meeting. Furthermore, the League favoured the law-abiding, peaceful methods of the NUWSS, rather than the law-breaking confrontational style of the WSPU, as the leaflet advertising their first public meeting in 1907 demonstrates:

1 We do not proceed by any uproarious methods; we content ourselves with appealing to the thoughtfulness of men, ... in this very slow moving country of ours no great movement can be carried through unless it is accompanied by what people at the time very likely think to be outra-
5 geous conduct ... we can do without it, because what we have to do is to show to the men voters in this country that the claim, the demand, the women are making is ... a claim which politically expediency ought to be only too ready to extend.[21]

Members of the League participated in demonstrations, wrote leaflets and pamphlets, organised petitions, lobbied MPs in support of women's suffrage and acted as a conduit between the suffragists and the government.

The second major organisation, the Men's Federation for Women's Suffrage, which was later renamed the Men's Political Union, was formally constituted in 1910. The Federation drew upon a more radical tradition than the League:

1 Firstly, the policy of this Union is action, entirely independent of political parties; secondly opposition to whatever government is in power, until such time as the franchise is granted; thirdly, participation in parliamentary elections in opposition to the government candidate, and
5 independently of all other candidates; and lastly, vigorous agitation and the education of public opinion by all the usual methods, such as public meetings, demonstrations, debates, distribution of literature, newspaper correspondence and deputations to public representatives.

The Federation identified more with the WSPU, using the same suffragette colours of purple, white and green, than with the NUWSS. It believed that if men were really anxious to help women achieve the vote they should sever all connections with party politics and devote their energies to the suffrage cause. There is no doubt that many men who belonged to the Federation gave much time and commitment to women's suffrage, combining traditional forms of protest with militant ones. The Federation helped organise demonstrations: for instance it helped the ELFS organise a march from the East End of

London to Trafalgar Square. When women were shut out of Liberal meetings, members of the Federation went in to represent them. It also heckled Liberal ministers: one man had his leg fractured in two places when he was thrown out of a meeting in Bradford. Another man attacked Winston Churchill with a whip; two more threw mouse traps at the MPs in Parliament from the Strangers' Gallery in protest at the Cat and Mouse Act; others broke windows; yet others attempted arson – Harold Laski, for example, tried (unsuccessfully) to destroy a railway station in 1913. As a result of these protests, men were imprisoned and, like women, went on hunger strike and were either released under the Cat and Mouse Act or else forcibly fed. One man who had set fire to a railway carriage was convicted, imprisoned and force-fed 114 times. Altogether 40 men were imprisoned for suffragette activities.

The WSPU initially welcomed this kind of male support, but by 1912 the Federation found itself out of favour with the WSPU. Indeed Emmeline Pethick-Lawrence stated that 'Men in prison only embarrass us.' As Sandra Holton points out, male violence was different from women's.[23] Firstly, she argues, female violence could be justified because women were excluded from traditional peaceful forms of political protest: because they had the vote, men could make their voices heard within the constitution. They had no need to resort to violence. Hence, Holton argues, male violence was seen by the WSPU to 'threaten the legitimacy of militant protest'. Secondly, suffragette militancy was justified by the suffragettes as part of a sex war with heroic, freedom-fighting women pitted against intransigent and violent men. The men who fought so hard for women's suffrage undermined this particular narrative because, as men, they were the enemy but, as members of the Federation, they were friends. Nevertheless, although exact figures are unknown, the number of men who joined the Federation was extremely small so the suffragettes were able to maintain their general beliefs about men.

As Brian Harrison points out, men also formed organisations to oppose women's suffrage. In 1909 a Men's League for Opposing Women's Suffrage was formed. It used similar tactics to the suffragists: they campaigned across the country, held meetings, collected signatures and raised funds. In some respects it did rather better than its opponents. During 1908 it collected 337,018 signatures against votes for women, whereas the suffragists only managed to obtain 288,736 a year later. Nevertheless, this group remained small, with a membership amounting to no more than 9000.

5 Conclusion

> **KEY ISSUES** How supportive were men of votes for women?

The suffrage movement may have received a mixed response from those men who belonged to formal organisations, but it was hopelessly unsuccessful in convincing the majority of British men. The evidence that is available – from famous individuals, from popular music hall songs, from the banning of women from certain places, and from the increasing level of violence in the crowds that gathered around women's demonstrations – points to a generally hostile reaction. However, it is difficult, if not impossible, to measure the extent to which these particular groups were representative of male opinion as a whole. In addition, research on the history of men and the suffrage movement remains sparse, making it hard to assess the level of either sympathy or hostility from men in general. It is tempting to suppose that the majority of men were apathetic and impartial rather than antagonistic but the evidence so far suggests that historians cannot make any very definite worthwhile judgements either way.

Historians claim that many aristocratic and upper-class men were opposed to votes for women. One famous doctor remarked in 1912 that 'there is mixed up with the women's movement much mental disorder'. London's male clubland generally opposed female suffrage, as did the Oxford Union. The royal family also opposed female suffrage: Edward VII was quite definitely against giving the vote to women. However, once again, these are just impressions based on a few individual comments and cannot be taken as representative of a whole social class.

Popular culture, in the form of Music hall songs and cartoons, offer entertaining insights into the minds of some men. The following popular songs are affectionate in tone but suggest that public opinion was negative:

Put me upon an island where the girls are few
Put me among the most ferocious lions in the zoo
Put me in a prison and I'll never never fret
But for pity's sake don't put me near a suffering-gette

Or

I'm suffering from a suffragette
Suffering all you can see
Since my wife joined the suffragettes
I have become a suffragee

Not all music hall artists were unsympathetic. After a short verse, one popular entertainer used to deliver a lengthy speech on the wrongs of women, urging them to stand up for their rights. Fear of militancy closed many of the country's art galleries and museums to the public completely or sometimes to women only. The rule of 'No muffs, wrist bags or sticks' was widespread: the Royal Academy and the Tate Gallery were closed to women and the British Museum announced that it was open to all men but only open to women if accompanied by men who were willing to vouch for their good behaviour. Unaccompanied women, they said, 'were only allowed in on presentation of a letter of introduction from a responsible person vouching for the bearer's good behaviour and accepting responsibility for her acts' (see the cartoon on page 95). Again, this response may be evidence of justifiable anxiety about the prospect of suffragette violence rather than of an unfriendly attitude.

Recent research indicates that many suffragettes were violently and indecently assaulted when they participated in demonstrations, campaigned at by-elections or heckled politicians. The occasions on which women had to put up with violent sexual harassment were numerous: they were often intimidated, attacked, and the victims of anti-suffrage rioting. Antagonistic men indecently assaulted women on demonstrations, ripping their clothes and whispering obscenities in their ears. Rosen has told of the number of men who came expressly to suffragette demonstrations to bully and sexually abuse women. Gangs of 'roughs' lay in wait for suffragettes who tried to get into the House of Commons. In Glasgow in March 1912, 200 men broke up the WSPU shop by throwing iron bolts and weights through the windows. At the Eisteddfod in Wales that year suffragettes who dared to heckle the local hero, Lloyd George, were seriously assaulted, their hair pulled and their clothing ripped – one woman was stripped to the waist, two women's shirts were cut up and the pieces given to the crowd. At another time the Croydon branch of the WSPU window was smashed and a WSPU stall in Walsall wrecked. Time and time again the suffragettes were subjected to brutal and sometimes sexual assault so that it became impossible for the WSPU to hold outdoor meetings because they feared violence by the crowd gathered to watch. Even Emmeline Pankhurst was not immune. When she opposed the Liberal candidate at Newton Abbot, Devon, Emmeline and her colleague were roughly handled and savagely assaulted by Liberal sympathisers. However, men who assaulted women were still very much in the minority, and so this type of harassment cannot be taken to indicate widespread male hostility to the suffrage.

Suffragists and suffragettes may have received an antagonistic response from some men but they drew support from unexpected quarters. Diane Atkinson has noted that many leading department stores, both in London and the provinces, displayed the WSPU colours in their windows. In 1908 in Lewisham, one large department store employed a WSPU speaker to address one of their sportsday events while Sainsburys' exhibited clothes of green, purple and white in their windows. Many other retail stores stocked clothes and other items in the suffragette colours. In 1910 the Votes for Women slogan was even printed on the wrappers of Allison's bread. This, of course, may have been just good business sense – the suffragettes were seen to be wealthy customers – but the displaying of suffragette colours may have antagonised more people than it attracted. Individual men continued to give support. In 1909 the journalists Henry Nevinson and H N Brailsford both resigned their jobs at the *Daily News* in protest. The cricketer Jack Hobbs, an East End prize fighter Kosher Hunt, and many middle-class intellectuals including Gilbert Murray, John Masefield and John Galsworthy all gave their support to the suffrage campaign.

There is still much more research needed on the relation of men to the women's suffrage movement but the history written so far has been affected by distinct social trends. At first, women's suffrage was subsumed under men's history: for example, George Dangerfield's book examines the suffrage movement as part of a general Liberal political decline. With the rise of a separate women's history in the 1970s, women's suffrage became part of that history with the result that the wider political debate was ignored. In a curious twist of historiography, suffrage history came to be built around the ultimately victorious female, with men largely eliminated from the story except as the implacable opposition. Just as women used to be hidden from men's history, so men today are hidden from women's suffrage history. Until 1997, when *The Men's Sphere* was published, there had virtually been no research on organised male support of suffrage, or the responses of religious organisations, or of newspaper coverage. Of course, histories that exclude these topics – like histories that exclude women – are not only inadequate but inaccurate because they portray only a partial view of the world. Historians must therefore question the *female* bias in suffrage history, *men's* invisibility, and argue for a reappraisal of history based on the experiences of both sexes.

Nonetheless, it is odd to write about men's involvement in what was essentially a women's movement. Men's support of the suffrage campaign certainly raises important questions about the traditional role of men and women. Men who supported the female franchise usually behaved in a supportive capacity to women. This of course is an interesting reversal of customary practice as it is usually women who take a back seat in political movements. What is more, even the men who opposed women's suffrage reacted to events rather than initiated them, a role reversal that, paradoxically, must have ultimately undermined their beliefs about women's role in society.

By the outbreak of war in 1914 the suffrage movement had reached an impasse. Although there were considerable numbers of men across the class, political and religious spectrums who supported women's suffrage, there were also considerable numbers who opposed it. Nevertheless, there was still a clear trend towards greater acceptance of the female vote. Parliament appeared little different from the nation at large in that MPs held a variety of opinions towards women's suffrage, ranging from sympathetic and indifferent to hostile. Liberal commitment to votes for women was muted, largely because of the intransigence of Asquith; Conservative opinion was generally opposed; while Labour was too insignificant a party to have much effect at all. It would take the trauma of war to break this particular deadlock.

References

1 *Leaflet of Conservative and Unionist Women's Franchise Association*, 27 April 1866.
2 *Leaflet of Conservative and Unionist Women's Franchise Association*, 12 November 1888.
3 *Leaflet of Conservative and Unionist Women's Franchise Association*, 27 April 1892.
4 *Hansard* May 1970 quoted in *The March of the Women*, Martin Pugh (Oxford University Press, 2000) p. 103.
5 *Women's Suffrage and Party Politics in Britain*, 1866–1914, Constance Rover (Routledge and Kegan Paul, 1967), p. 120.
6 'In the Comradeship of the Sexes Lies the Hope of Progress and Social Regeneration: Women in the West Riding ILP, c.1890–1914' by June Hannam in *Equal or Different*, J. Rendal (ed) (Basil Blackwell, 1987), p. 230.
7 *Ramsay MacDonald*, David Marquand (Jonathan Cape, 1977), p. 148.
8 Mrs Matilda Mullins, (No 25) aged 60, Suffragette Testimonies from Museum of London Suffragette Collection.
9 *Rise Up Women: The Militant Campaign of the WSPU 1903–1914*, A. Rosen (Routledge and Kegan Paul, 1974), p. 145.
10 *Independent Women*, Martha Vicinus (Routledge, 1985), p. 261.
11 'The Prison Experiences of the Suffragettes in Edwardian Britain' by June Purvis, *Women's History Review*, vol. 4, no. 1, 1995.
12 Ibid.
13 *One Hand Tied Behind Us*, Jill Liddington and Jill Norris (Virago, 1978) p. 150.
14 Leaflet printed by the WSPU c. 1912.
15 WSPU Annual Report, 1914.
16 *Opinions of Leaders of Religious Thought* (Central Society for Women's Suffrage, 1905), p. 10.
17 *Separate Spheres: The Opposition to Women's Suffrage in Britain*, Brian Harrison (Croom Helm, 1978) p. 33.
18 Ibid, p. 28.
19 Ibid, p. 28.
20 Laura Ugolini, in, *The Men's Share*, Angela John and Clare Eustance (Routledge, 1997), p. 73.
21 *Yours in the Cause*, Iris Dove (Lewisham Library Service and Greenwich Library, 1988), p. 10.
22 Leaflet of Men's League for Women's Suffrage, December 1907.
23 Sandra Stanley Holton in *The Men's Share*, p. 15.

Summary Diagram

Men and votes for women

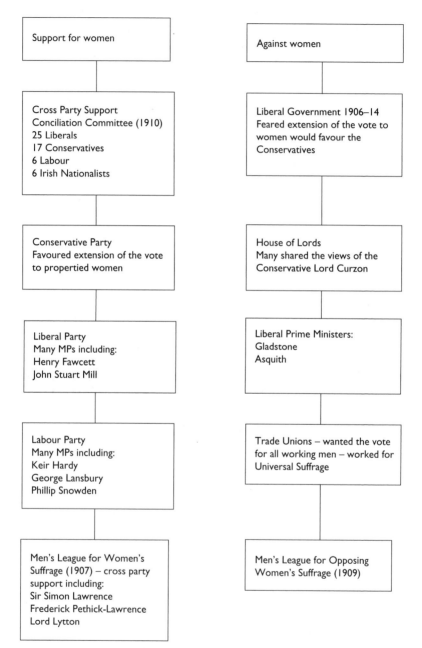

Support for women

Cross Party Support
Conciliation Committee (1910)
25 Liberals
17 Conservatives
6 Labour
6 Irish Nationalists

Conservative Party
Favoured extension of the vote
to propertied women

Liberal Party
Many MPs including:
Henry Fawcett
John Stuart Mill

Labour Party
Many MPs including:
Keir Hardy
George Lansbury
Phillip Snowden

Men's League for Women's
Suffrage (1907) – cross party
support including:
Sir Simon Lawrence
Frederick Pethick-Lawrence
Lord Lytton

Against women

Liberal Government 1906–14
Feared extension of the vote to
women would favour the
Conservatives

House of Lords
Many shared the views of the
Conservative Lord Curzon

Liberal Prime Ministers:
Gladstone
Asquith

Trade Unions – wanted the vote
for all working men – worked for
Universal Suffrage

Men's League for Opposing
Women's Suffrage (1909)

Working on Chapter 5

This chapter covers some of the reasons for male opposition to women and the right to vote. You should now understand that the response of men to votes for women was more than 'a battle between the sexes'. When the Liberal Government was elected in 1906 with a large majority in the House of Commons many believed that electoral reform including votes for women would be achieved. However, as this chapter outlines, the struggle was nowhere near being won, in fact female suffrage appeared to take a step backwards. In your notes you need to identify why the decision was delayed. When reading the chapter keep the following questions in mind:

- Was Asquith solely responsible for delaying votes for women?
- How supportive was Lloyd George?
- What about the actions of the leaders of the Labour Party and the Trade Unions?

Answering structured questions and essay questions on Chapter 5

This phase of the struggle for the right to vote is characterised by the increased militancy of the suffragettes and the reaction of the Liberal Governments to this. It also highlights the complexity of the struggle in terms of male support for women's right to vote and how this support came from across the classes and political parties. The usual approach with structured questions is to ask a relatively straightforward first part, followed by more demanding questions later. Look at the following examples:

1 **a)** In what ways did the Liberal Government's treatment of the suffragettes differ to that of the Ulster Unionists? (8 marks)
   b) Why was women's suffrage held back in the years 1906–14? (12 marks)
2 **a)** Explain briefly why sections of the trade union movement withheld their support for female suffrage? (8 marks)
   b) How did the Liberal Government undermine the efforts of the women's suffrage movement in the years 1906–14? (12 marks)

The following are example of essay questions:

1 Despite a large majority in the House of Commons why did the Liberal Governments of 1906–14 continue to oppose women's suffrage? (15 marks)
2 Do you agree with the view that the militancy of the suffragettes was the reason why Parliament refused to enfranchise women in the years 1906–14? (15 marks)
3 Why did the Conciliation Committee fail to get support for their Bills in the House of Commons in the years 1910–12? (15 marks)

When, for example, you are making a plan to answer Question 3, draw up a list of the problems the Committee faced. Opposite each one note the extent to which it dealt with the problem. Now list the reasons for the failure of the Bills. What connection do they have with the lack of success.

Answering source based questions on Chapter 5

1 Liberal Legislation:
Read and examine the sources 'Puss in Boots' and the extract from *The Lancet* 12 August 1912 on page 89. Answer the following questions:
  a) What can you learn from 'Puss in Boots' about the reaction of the press to the 'Cat and Mouse Act' of 1913? (*4 marks*)
  b) Explain why Parliament passed the 'Cat and Mouse Act in April 1913. (*6 marks*)
  c) In what ways do 'Puss in Boots' and the article in *The Lancet* differ in their view of the forced feeding of the suffragettes? How do you account for these differences? (*12 marks*)
  d) Compare the value of these two sources as evidence for the historian enquiring into the role of the suffragettes in gaining the vote for women. (*12 marks*)
2 Church and press views of the suffragette struggle:
Read and examine the extract from the speech by the Rector of Whitburn on page 93 and look at the cartoon in the *Daily Mirror* on page 95
  a) What does the *Daily Mirror* cartoon published in 1914 suggest about the responses of museum to women visitors? (*4 marks*)
  b) How useful are the two sources to an historian investigating support for women's suffrage in the years 1906–14? (*6 marks*)
  c) To what extent do the sources provide an understanding of the nature of support for women's Suffrage? (*12 marks*)

Note that part **c)** of each question is asking you to evaluate the sources either regarding their differences or their contribution to understanding much wider issues. It is important that you are critical in your response. Stress limitations as well as strengths.

6 Women, Suffrage and the First World War

POINTS TO CONSIDER

The Great War is often seen as a turning point in suffrage history. Shortly after war was declared on Germany in August 1914 most of the women's suffrage groups abandoned their campaign for the vote in favour of supporting the war effort. This chapter will examine suffrage responses to the war and the work of the various groups on behalf of the war effort. By the end of the chapter you should be able to decide the extent to which women achieved the vote as a result of their work in the First World War.

KEY DATES

1914   August Britain declared war on Germany; amnesty for suffragettes
1915   Asquith forms Coalition Government; Right to work march; Munitions Act
1916   Speaker's Conference; Lloyd George becomes Prime Minister; Demonstration of war workers
1918   Representation of the People Act gave votes for women over the age of 30; Armistice with Germany signed

The First World War had a profound effect on suffrage politics. In August 1914, as Britain was going to war against Germany, the WSPU declared peace with the Liberals – the sex war, as Martin Pugh has pointed out, was swamped by the Great War. In one of her characteristic aphorisms, Emmeline Pankhurst remarked that there was no point in continuing to fight for the vote when there might be no country to vote in. The rest of the major suffrage societies agreed with her, discontinued their suffrage campaign and shifted their energies to support the war effort.

However, it has been argued that the greatest effect of the war on women's suffrage was that women were granted the vote towards the end of it. On 6 February 1918, 8 million women, out of an electorate of 21 million, were given the opportunity to vote. Until fairly recently, historians generally agreed that women were awarded the vote as a token of gratitude for their war work. 'The highly skilled and dangerous work done by women during the war in the armament and munitions factories and in auxiliary and nursing service at the Front was probably the greatest factor in the granting of the vote to women at the end of the war.'[1] Yet the evidence for this interpretation is inconclusive and several historians have questioned the direct correlation between women's war work and women's suffrage. They argue that the emphasis placed on women's economic contribution to the war discounts the groundwork put in by the pre-war suffrage campaign. To complicate matters, a few historians have even suggested that the war, far from facilitating votes for women, actually postponed its implementation. Women's suffrage, they suggest, was on the verge of being granted just before the war broke out. This chapter will explore these controversies, examine the responses of the suffrage movement towards the war and consider the reasons for the success of women's suffrage in 1918.

1 The Suffrage Movement and the War

> **KEY ISSUE** What kinds of contribution did the women's suffrage movement make to the war effort?

It may seem reasonable to suppose that both the suffragettes and the suffragists helped women gain the vote by leading their organisations to support the war effort. Yet, while this is a plausible explanation, it is only partially valid as the response of the women's suffrage movement to war was varied. Certainly, the WSPU led the way in patriotism, followed less enthusiastically by the NUWSS. But what is noticeable in the histories of the suffrage movement during the war is that others were reluctant to support what was perceived as an imperialist war. However, it is perfectly safe to say that, at the least, war brought suffrage activity to a sudden halt.

a) The Women's Social and Political Union

When war was declared in August 1914 the WSPU suspended suffrage activities and called upon its members to support the war effort. Emmeline Pankhurst and her daughter, Christabel, saw the war, just as they had the suffrage question, as the 'goodies' fighting the 'baddies', as a battle between the enlightened democracy of Britain and the autocratic militarism of Wilhelmine Germany. Germany – like their previous enemy the Liberal Government – was depicted as the world's bully who overrode every principle of humanity and morality and whose unbridled aggression had provoked the war in the first place. At a meeting held at the London Opera House in September 1914, Christabel Pankhurst extolled the virtues of living under the British system and pleaded for Britain to support the 'feminine' state of France that had been threatened by the 'over-masculine state' of Germany.[2] God, according to the Pankhursts, was firmly on the British side. Ironically, one of their greatest principles, that of the unity of women, disappeared at a stroke under the cloak of nationalism.

So, at the outbreak of war the WSPU and its members abandoned their violent methods and demonstrated a new patriotic loyalty.

Within a few days of war, Emmeline Pankhurst threw herself into a vigorous campaign in which the defeat of Germany took priority over women's suffrage. And with somewhat alarming alacrity, the WSPU placed its organisation, and its funds, at the disposal of the Government, which by 1915 was desperate to recruit women workers. From 1915 onwards there was a great shortage of labour: 2 million men had joined the armed forces at a time of pressing demand for increased munition production. To encourage women to join the workforce, Lloyd George, now Minister of Munitions, liaised with the WSPU. Enmities between the two were quickly overcome. Demonstrations, largely financed by Lloyd George and co-ordinated by the WSPU, were organised to publicise the need for women to join the labour force. For example, the WSPU was given £2000 to stage a 'women's right to serve' march (known as The Great Procession of Women), on 17 July 1915. This demonstration used all the theatricality of the suffragette marches of the past but with a new twist: Emmeline sat in a car decked out in white, red and blue instead of the old WSPU colours and women from the various allied countries carried their national flag, while each British contingent held the Union Jack instead of a votes for women banner.

The jingoism of the leaders of the WSPU matched that of the general public. Shedding their subversive, and somewhat anarchistic, role of the pre-war years, the suffragettes became arch-patriots. In 1915 the suffragettes renamed their paper *Britannia* to express their commitment to the British Empire, and in November 1917 the name of the WSPU was changed to the Women's Party. Emmeline and Christabel Pankhurst set about promoting the war effort world-wide: they launched a campaign to urge Russian women to encourage their men to keep fighting and toured America and Canada to speak on women and war service. At home, they called for military conscription for men, industrial conscription for women and the abolition of trade unions. Furthermore, the WSPU demanded that conscientious objectors, alongside those of the enemy race living in Britain, be interned. Emmeline Pankhurst once again toured the country, this time to encourage men to work hard for the war effort and to recruit women for the munition factories.

Yet not all WSPU members agreed with the Pankhurst pronouncements and their use of WSPU funds to promote the war effort. As a consequence, two different groups split from the WSPU to form their own suffrage organisations: the Suffragettes of the Women's Social and Political Union (SWSPU) in October 1915 and the Independent Women's Social and Political Union (IWSPU) in March 1916. Unfortunately, apart from a brief mention in a few books, these groups have largely been ignored by historians. However, each group produced its own paper, the *Suffragette News Sheet* and *The Independent Suffragette*, which provide some opportunities for historical research.

b) The East London Federation of Suffragettes and the Women's Freedom League

In marked contrast to her flag-waving relatives, Sylvia Pankhurst condemned the war as an imperialistic venture, supported conscientious objection, adhered to her socialist principles and emerged as 'one of Britain's leading revolutionary anti-war agitators'.[3] At times the ELFS even preached sedition. 'We believe that the conscientious objector who refuses to become a soldier, the soldiers who establish a truce in the trenches, and the people which forces its Government to make peace, are all fighting the same fight'.[4] In the midst of war the ELFS published a letter from the leader of the Social Democrats in Germany, Karl Liebkneckt, urging suffragettes to fight both for the vote and for peace. Sylvia Pankhurst also participated in a Women's Peace Conference at The Hague and was elected to the Executive Committee of the Women's International League. By the end of the war she was a fully fledged revolutionary socialist who believed that only a complete change in society could herald equality between the sexes. She, and her organisation, applauded the Bolshevik revolution in Russia because 'the capitalist system of society is irreconcilable with the freedom and the just demands of the workers'.[5] She urged the abolition of capitalism and called for the establishment of a Socialist Commonwealth. It is therefore not surprising that in 1916 the ELFS first changed its name to the Workers' Suffrage Federation and later in 1918 to the Workers' Socialist Federation with a corresponding change in their newspaper title from *The Women's Dreadnought* to *The Workers' Dreadnought* in 1917.

Throughout the war Sylvia and the ELFS campaigned for civil liberties, for the control of food prices and profits and for the nationalisation of the food supply. They railed against rising food prices. Towards the end of the war they demanded the abolition of private profit, the socialisation of food and even suggested that food be supplied free, paid for by the rates. The plight of working-class women also concerned the ELFS and much of its effort revolved around improving their lives. The ELFS campaigned for better rates of pay in charitable organisations such as Queen Mary's Workshops; sent petitions, demonstrations and deputations concerning pay and conditions in munitions factories to Lloyd George; and supported equal pay for equal work, arguing that it was 'vitally important that every woman shall refuse to do a man's work unless she gets a man's pay'.[6] When the Government introduced Regulation 40D (which made it a crime for women with venereal disease to have, or even suggest to have, sexual intercourse with anyone in the armed forces), the ELFS, along with other feminist groups, opposed it. In this they were unsuccessful.

The war brought distress to soldiers' wives and dependants and so the ELFS campaigned widely on their behalf. In 1914 it protested against the 'Cessation of Separation Allowances and of Allotments of Pay to the Unworthy', which threatened to discontinue the allowances of women found guilty of misconduct, immorality or child neglect. In 1915, along with the local Labour MP, George Lansbury, the ELFS also formed the League of Rights for Soldiers and Sailors' Wives and Relatives to fight for an increase in the separation allowances paid to women whose husbands were away fighting.

From the evidence charted above, and the fact that it was a tiny organisation, it is difficult to believe that the government wished to reward the ELFS for their emphatically negative reaction to the war. However, in much of its practice, the ELFS mirrored the work of other suffrage organisations by focusing on relief work. For much of the time Sylvia Pankhurst acted as social worker rather than working socialist. She, and her organisation, opened an unemployment bureau and set up a toy and boot factory to help the unemployed. The ELFS set up five centres in the East End of London, which offered free milk to mothers and a nurse to advise on the health of their babies; it converted an old pub called the Gunmakers' Arms into a nursery and renamed it the Mothers' Arms; and it opened a cost-price restaurant that offered dinner at 2d, well below the price charged by local restaurants. This restaurant was used regularly by East Enders but it was often criticised because the food it served – such as unpeeled potatoes and unpeeled turnips – although healthy, looked unappetising.

Charlotte Despard, leader of the Women's Freedom League (WFL) shared Sylvia Pankhurst's belief that the war was an imperialist venture. These two ardent socialists remained convinced of the need for international solidarity and rejected the overwhelming, and to their eyes, unthinking patriotism of their former colleagues. The fact that Despard's brother was Chief of Staff of the British Army and Commander of the British Expeditionary Force did not deter her from becoming active in the peace campaign. In her view the British government had not done enough to avoid war so she supported the campaign of the Women's Peace Council for a negotiated peace. Unfortunately the members of the WFL disagreed with her politics, disassociated themselves from her position and declared that Despard's pacifism was in no way representative of their organisation.

c) The National Union of Women's Suffrage Societies

Meanwhile the NUWSS was bitterly divided over the war. While there were some members who wholeheartedly supported the war effort, there were others who were ambivalent and still others who were unwilling to support it at all. Millicent Fawcett represented the first group believing that 'a wholesome internationalism could rest only on a wholesome nationalism'.[7] Although she had signed an appeal for peace at the beginning of August 1914 she changed her mind a few days later when war broke out and declared 'Women, your country needs you'. War, she believed, was the gravest crisis facing Britain, for if Germany won it would destroy the democratic institution of Parliament. Nonetheless, Millicent Fawcett 'was no flag waving jingoist; she opposed the idea of giving white feathers ... regretted the need for conscription and repudiated vulgar anti-German feeling'.[8] Indeed, she regretted the war but felt it impolitic to implicate suffrage with the controversy over pacifism versus patriotism.

Not all members of the NUWSS agreed with Fawcett, preferring to retain their identity as suffragists rather than be swept away by a wave of chauvinism. Eventually these disagreements led to a division in the NUWSS, especially when it refused official recognition to an international Peace Conference for women held at The Hague. Millicent Fawcett, in particular, refused to associate the NUWSS with the conference because she feared that its reputation would be damaged if it was associated with pacifism. In the end all the national officers, apart from Millicant Fawcett and the Treasurer, resigned to form the Women's International League for Peace and Freedom.

Whatever their attitude towards the war almost all of the suffragists were active in wartime relief work. Indeed relief work served to heal some of the divisions within the NUWSS and strengthened the bonds between the remaining membership. One of the first tasks of the NUWSS was to establish a register of voluntary workers, who would in turn find suitable work for the unemployed. When war broke out there was a dramatic increase in female unemployment as many of the industries such as dressmaking, which employed large numbers of women, virtually collapsed as richer women cut back on their purchase of luxury goods. Other industries failed as well, leaving many women out of work. For example, cotton, when the German market ended, and fisheries, when the North Sea was closed to shipping. By September 1914 over 44 per cent of women were unemployed.

In response to this high female unemployment, members of the NUWSS set to work organising the unemployed and soon became the major focus of relief work in many cities and towns. In Birmingham, it opened a workroom where garments were made for war relief and a dining room for pregnant and nursing mothers as well as establishing women patrols to 'protect the honour of young girls' and guard against prostitution. At the outbreak of war the Dundee branch offered to help the city council alleviate poverty and distress caused by war; similarly the Edinburgh and Glasgow branches undertook relief work. In London, the NUWSS established a Women's Service Bureau that worked with Belgian refugees, War Relief Committees, Red Cross Units, Hospital Stores and Canteens.

By 1915 there was a shortage of workers, so the NUWSS set up an employment register and interviewed women to replace the men sent to the front. For example, the first 80 munition workers at the Woolwich Arsenal were recruited by the London Society, as were supervisors and workers for munition factories all over Britain.

Training schools, like the one for oxyacetylene welding at Notting Hill, were also opened by the London branch to supply workers for the aircraft industry.

One of the most important initiatives of the NUWSS was the setting up and financing of Scottish Women's Hospitals Units. These units employed all-female teams of doctors, nurses and ambulance drivers to work on the front lines of the war in some of the worst of the fighting zones. By 1915 there were five medical units operating in Corsica, France, Salonika and Serbia. The NUWSS also provided medical relief for groups of civilians in different parts of Europe who had been disturbed by the upheaval of war. Under a predominantly Quaker aegis, maternity and children's hospitals were set up for refugees and sanatoria for tuberculosis sufferers.

Unlike the WSPU, the NUWSS remained committed to women's suffrage. It left its organisational structure intact so that it would be in a position to recommence suffrage activities when the time was right. Indeed the NUWSS used the same staff and organising facilities for its relief work as it had for the vote. Some branches, such as Birmingham's, never lost sight of the suffrage cause and held meetings and demonstrations and drafted petitions to promote votes for women. This was significant, for whenever the franchise question was raised in the House of Commons the NUWSS was well placed to lobby trade unions, municipal authorities, the press and the Government in support of women's suffrage. More importantly, the hard work of both

Women aircraft workers in the First World War.

the suffragettes and the suffragists during the war ended the spectre of militancy and conferred respectability on the suffrage cause. It was thought that the women involved in the suffrage movement had shown themselves to be responsible and mature beings who were more than capable of taking part in the democracy that they had worked hard to defend.

2 Women's War Work and the Vote

> **KEY ISSUE** To what extent did women gain the vote because of their war work?

When women were enfranchised in 1918 billboards announced that 'The Nation Thanks the Women' – as if a grateful nation, over-whelmed by the sacrifices of munition workers in particular, was now granting them suffrage as reward for their efforts. Or was it that women were now being enfranchised because the war had changed masculine perceptions about women's role in society? Now, for the first time women were accepted in the public world of work, and this acceptance led, ultimately, to their participation in the public world of politics.

From the outset women of all social classes were absorbed into the war effort and played a crucial part on the home front. Many upper-class and middle-class women experienced their first taste of paid work during the war, entering occupations that would have been deemed unsuitable in peacetime. Aristocratic women were found in the higher echelons, advising government departments on health and employment, heading Food Economy Campaigns, and presiding over the newly formed women's armed services. Lady Londonderry, for example, became the first Colonel in Chief of the Women's Volunteer Reserve in February 1915. Two years later, when the Land Army was formed, women from upper- and middle-class backgrounds joined as agricultural workers. (Selection boards usually turned down working-class women who volunteered for the Land Army because they were believed to lack the high moral fibre needed for farm life.) On the farm, women were expected to do a wide variety of jobs such as ploughing, planting and harvesting as well as look after the sheep and other animals.

Other women joined the Women's Auxiliary Army Corps (WAACS) which had been formed in 1916, the Women's Royal Naval Service (WRENS), or the Women's Royal Air Force (WRAFS), set up in 1918. Most women who joined the auxiliary armed forces worked in a supportive capacity, as drivers, messengers, typists, telephonists and storekeepers but some did receive technical training. A few WRAFS were employed as welders and carpenters to work on aeroplanes but none actually flew so they were called penguins: birds who cannot fly. The *Daily Express* once suggested that flying should not be a woman's job because they would lose their heads in an emergency! Although not officially enlisted, these women were considered part of the regular British Army. And at the very least, as Martin Pugh notes, the war disposed of one old argument against votes for women – the one that women were incapable of taking part in the defence of the country. Undoubtedly women did play a large part in the nation's defence – at least on the home front – and were certainly entitled to benefit from the consequences.

Upper-class women also joined the Voluntary Aid Detachment (VAD). This was formed in 1909 but was greatly expanded during the war, to nurse injured soldiers both at home and at the front. These women have often been portrayed romantically as heroines who sacrificed their privileged upbringing to nurse the sick and wounded. Vera Brittain (a famous writer and mother of former MP Shirley Williams), who was about to go to Oxford when war was declared, wrote about her experiences as a young VAD gazing 'half-hypnotized, at the dishevelled beds, the stretchers on the floor, the scattered boots and piles of muddy khaki, the brown blankets turned back from smashed limbs bound to splints by filthy blood-stained bandages. Beneath each stinking wad of sodden wool and gauze an obscene horror waited for me.'[9] Criticism was sometimes made of these middle-class girls who perhaps spent a morning at the hospital whilst domestic servants cleaned their homes. Nevertheless, these nurses generally received a sympathetic press and were seen to deserve the vote.

Unlike most of their upper- and middle-class colleagues, working-class women did not go out to work because of the war. They had to work anyway. However, war did change the nature of their occupation. War offered an alternative to the grossly exploitative job in domestic service or sweated labour. In fact domestic service diminished by 400,000 during the war, reducing from 1,658,000 to 1,258,000. At railway stations there were women porters, ticket collectors and guards. Women replaced men as bus drivers, window cleaners, chimney sweeps, coal deliverers, street sweepers, electricians and fire-fighters. By 1917 bus conductresses had gone up from a half a dozen to about 2500 and female transport workers increased from 18,000 in 1914 to 117,000 in 1918. Munitions obviously showed the biggest increase. In 1914 Woolwich Arsenal employed 125 women whereas by 1917 over 25,000 women worked there.

It was the munition worker who captured the imagination of the press and the general public. Munition workers performed a variety of jobs, ranging from filling shells and making bullets to assembling detonators. Their hours were long – sometimes 14 hours a day for weeks on end – and their conditions of work known to be dangerous. TNT poisoning, which turned the skin yellow thus earning the women the nickname of 'Canary Girls', was an occupational hazard. In Woolwich Arsenal about 37 per cent of the women suffered from stomach pain, nausea and constipation as a result of TNT poisoning. Other symptoms included skin rashes, giddiness, drowsiness and swelling of hands and feet. In 1916 the first deaths from toxic jaundice were reported but little was done. Working in a munition factory was made highly dangerous by the risk of explosion. Safety measures were taken to avoid accidents: each woman had to hand over all personal belongings such as matches, cigarettes, wedding rings and other jewellery before they entered the shell filling section. Women wore protective clothes without any metal zips in them, garters rather than suspender belts and caps to tie up long hair as metal hair grips were banned. In spite of these precautions accidents were common. The most notorious was at Silvertown in the East End of London in 1917 where a number of women were killed in an horrific explosion.

3 War, Suffrage and the Government

> **KEY ISSUES** Why do you think the Government began to support suffrage? What were the factors that caused it to change its policy on the issue?

It is important, of course, to examine women's suffrage and war from the perspective of parliamentary politics. For over 50 years before the war an all-male Parliament had been reluctant to enfranchise women and yet by the close of war in 1918 politicians had changed their minds. The reasons for the shifts that took place in Government thinking between 1914 and 1918 therefore need consideration.

Perhaps most importantly, there was a need for franchise reform in general. The existing franchise law required men who qualified as householders to have occupied a dwelling for at least a year prior to an election. Large numbers of the armed forces were thus ineligible to vote because they no longer held or had never held a 12-month residency. And a significant minority of men, who had risked their lives fighting in the front lines, had never ever been enfranchised. This, of course, would not do. In 1916, an all-party conference, composed of MPs from both the House of Commons and the House of Lords presided over by the Speaker of the House of Commons, was appointed to draft a proposal on the franchise and registration. The Speaker's Conference, as it was known, took place behind closed doors, no evidence was gathered and no lobbying accepted. The debate was conducted without any contribution from women – at least officially. Fortunately, there were many supporters of women's suffrage within the Speaker's Conference, so arguments in favour of votes for women were assured of a sympathetic hearing. In the end a limited number of women were granted the vote: women over the age of 30 who were either on the local government register or married to men on the local government register – because it was feared that if women were given the vote on exactly the same terms as men they might swamp the male electorate. Nevertheless, over 8 million women were enfranchised.

Moreover, there were a number of key changes in Parliament that altered the balance between those who opposed and those who were in favour of votes for women. The appointment of several suffragist MPs to Government posts augured well for the success of any women's suffrage amendment. Balfour, Bonar Law and Arthur Henderson, all of whom supported suffrage, were also promoted to the Cabinet replacing men who were antagonistic. More importantly Lloyd George, who was (more or less) sympathetic to women's suffrage, replaced Asquith as Prime Minister in December 1916. Lloyd George encouraged the previously unsympathetic newspaper *The Times* to carry glowing articles on women war workers to add weight to women's suffrage and influence wavering and antagonistic MPs.

The war allowed a number of hostile MPs – Asquith in particular – the excuse to climb down from their, now untenable, position of opposing votes for women. These MPs, although not fully converted to women's suffrage, realised that reform was inevitable and so used women's war work as a pretext to recant and save face. Women, so they rationalised, had demonstrated that they were mature and sensible enough to be rewarded with the vote by their significant contribution towards the war effort. As Asquith stated, somewhat disengenuously given his previous comments about women's suffrage, in 1917:

1   Why, and in what sense, the House may ask, have I changed my views? … My opposition to woman suffrage has always been based, and based solely, on considerations of public expediency. I think that some years ago I ventured to use the expression 'Let the women work out their
5   own salvation'. Well, Sir, they have … How could we have carried on the War without them? There is hardly a service in which women have not been at least as active as men … But what moves me more in this matter is the problem of reconstruction when the war is over. The questions which will arise with regard to women's labour and women's
10   functions are questions in which I find it impossible to withhold from women, the power and the right of making their voices heard. And let me add that, since the War began, now nearly three years ago, we have had no recurrence of that detestable campaign which disfigured the annals of political agitation in this country, and no one can now contend
15   that we are yielding to violence what we refused to concede to argument.

But his private remarks concerning the female electorate of Paisley in 1920 suggest that he still resented women's involvement in parliamentary politics:

> There are about fifteen thousand women on the Register – a dim, impenetrable lot, for the most part hopelessly ignorant of politics, credulous to the last degree, and flickering with gusts of sentiment like a candle in the wind.

In May 1915 the Liberal Government evolved into a Coalition government. The resulting decline in the importance of party divisions offered the prospect of all-party agreement on women's suffrage. As Brian Harrison points out, women's suffrage supporters were no longer fragmented between two, and sometimes three, political parties. Furthermore, the old fears that one party might benefit from women's suffrage were laid to rest. The enfranchisement of some 8 million women did not present an advantage to any one political party. On the one hand, both the Liberals and the Labour Party thought that the new proposed female electorate was much too large and socially mixed to give any advantage to the Conservatives. On the other hand, the Conservatives recognised that by this time adult male suffrage was unavoidable and so had little to lose – and perhaps something to gain – by women over 30, who were thought to be politically moderate, being included. The fact that munition workers in the main were excluded from the vote was also significant in gaining Conservative support. Munition workers were of course predominantly working-class and under 30 and might have voted Labour. Women's suffrage was therefore a compromise: no party got exactly what it wanted. Like other reform Acts it was illogical – there was no rational justification for excluding younger women, especially when younger male conscripts received the vote. Nonetheless, the compromise worked because it maximised support when the more radical proposal of universal suffrage might not.

Finally, Britain was merely reflecting an international trend towards full democracy. Women in New Zealand, Australia, Finland, Denmark and Norway had already been enfranchised. Canada (except Quebec) had granted votes for women in 1917 as had four American states. And just as the debate was taking place on women's suffrage in Britain, the American House of Representatives carried votes for women by a two-thirds majority (even though it was not ratified until August 1920). It would have been a peculiar political embarrassment if Britain – the mother of democracy – lagged behind those offspring countries.

As a consequence, when the division bell sounded in the House of Commons, 385 MPs voted in favour and 55 against the clause in the Representation of the People Bill supporting votes for women. The Bill then passed smoothly through the Lords largely because Lord Curzon, member of the Coalition Government and President of the League for Opposing Woman Suffrage, encouraged peers to abstain from voting if they could not support it. And so, on 6 February 1918, votes for women – after more than 60 years of campaigning and a war to end all wars – was at last achieved.

4 Conclusion

> **KEY ISSUE** Why did women gain the vote in 1918?

It would be naive to believe that women received the vote solely for services rendered in the First World War. It must be remembered that only women over 30 were given the vote (see page 115) and these were not people who had made the most substantial contribution towards the country's defence. Indeed the very women who had helped in the war effort – the young women of the munitions factories in particular – were actually denied the vote. As Martin Pugh has noted, the vote – as in the Second Reform Act – was conferred on the respectable and the responsible. It was felt unlikely that responsible married women would commit themselves to radical demands or revolutionary change but instead would help promote social stability amongst younger women. Unrest was a real fear since post-war Britain was threatened by widespread strike action, even by the police force. There were mutinies in the army and even an organisation that mirrored the Bolsheviks: the Leeds Soviet Convention that called for the creation of workers' and soldiers' councils. Older women, it was felt, might help stave off the riots and revolutions that were seen to menace the country by being a steadying voice in the political arena. Moreover, as men returned from fighting in the trenches they wanted their jobs back in the factories, in transport and in offices. In 1918 a trade union conference called for women to be banned from 'unsuitable' trades, for their hours to be regulated and for the exclusion of married women from work. Women's jobs in the war were not, and were never meant to be, permanent. However, women had tasted economic independence and may well have been ambivalent about returning to the domestic hearth – the vote therefore may have cushioned the Government from female complaints about injustice.

Of course, women might well not have been granted the vote if the suffragists and suffragettes had not campaigned so effectively before the war. Undoubtedly, the pre-war suffrage movement did much to prepare the ground for votes for women. French women, by contrast, were not enfranchised despite their participation in the war effort, largely because there had been no women's suffrage movement pre-war. Furthermore, it seemed likely that the women's suffrage movement would recommence once the war had ended with perhaps a renewal of the militancy that had plagued previous governments. One can only assume that, because the political climate was very different in 1918 than it had been in 1914, it would be inconceivable for the Government to imprison those self-same women who had so publicly participated in the war effort. As Morgan suggests, 'it was clear that the killing of Suffrage by any method would lead to a dangerous reversion to massive dissatisfaction among thousands of women whom publicly politicians were praising for their war efforts'.[10] And this was at a time of widespread strikes and a fear of Bolshevism.

It is possible that the war actually delayed the granting of the franchise. Just before the outbreak of war there were conciliatory gestures by key MPs: Asquith received deputations from the NUWSS and the ELFS; Sir John Simon, an influential member of the Cabinet, came out in support; and Lloyd George offered a place on his platform to suffrage speakers. There was also evidence to suggest that the Liberal Party was pressurising prospective MPs to support women's suffrage and replacing those unsympathetic to the suffrage cause with those who agreed with it. Holton argues that 'only two weeks before the outbreak of war, negotiations between suffragists and government were taking place'.[11] In addition, the Liberal leadership seemed ready to make women's suffrage part of its party programme. These, of course, must remain tentative speculations. Negotiations between the government and women's suffragists had taken place many times before but had never provided votes for women. There was no guarantee that it would have been the case this time.

Clearly, neither the view that women achieved the vote entirely because of their pre-war campaigns nor the view that women achieved the vote solely because of the war is ultimately sustainable. As with most historical judgements, there are a number of reasons for such a significant event and historians much prefer a synthesis of causes to crude over-simplification. It must also be remembered that the vote was still not entirely won: full adult universal suffrage was not achieved until 1928.

References

1 *Eva Gore Booth and Esther Roper*, Gifford Lewis (Pandora, 1988), pp. 165–6.
2 *Prudent Revolutionaries*, Brian Harrison (Clarendon Press, 1987), p. 35.
3 *Sylvia Pankhurst*, Barbara Winslow (UCL, 1996), p. 76.
4 *Workers' Dreadnought*, 17 August 1917.
5 Ibid, 2 June 1917.
6 *Woman's Dreadnought*, 13 February 1915.
7 *Prudent Revolutionaries*, Brian Harrison (Clarendon Press, 1987), p. 18.
8 Ibid.
9 *Testament of Youth*, Vera Brittain (Virago, 1992), p. 410.
10 *Suffragists and Liberals*, D Morgan (Blackwell, 1975), p. 143.
11 *Suffrage and Democracy*, Sandra Stanley Holton (Cambridge University Press, 1986) p. 125.

Summary Diagram
Women, Suffrage and the First World War

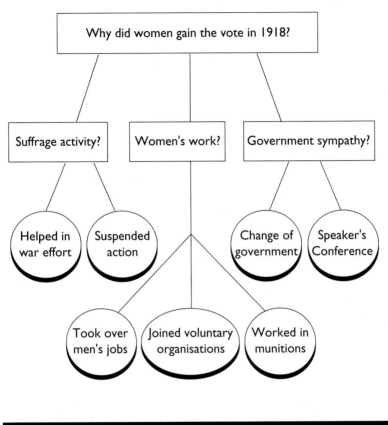

| | Working on Chapter 6 | |

The First World War is often seen as a turning point in suffrage history. Shortly after war was declared most of the women's suffrage groups suspended their campaigns. However, not all the members of the WSPU and NUWSS were in favour of the war. Millicent Fawcett, whilst not totally against the war, choose not to support the Women's League for Freedom, whereas most of the officers of the NUWSS helped to form the League. The WSPU was similarly divided with Sylvia Pankhurst supporting the Women's League of Freedom, whereas Christabel and Emmeline gave wholehearted support to Lloyd George's campaigns to mobilise women. The key issue to consider when reading this chapter is to what extent were women given the vote as a result of their war work. For this you need to understand exactly what women contributed to the war effort, the changes in government and the need for electoral revision. You may also consider whether or not the war delayed rather than hastened the extension of the franchise.

Answering structured questions and essay questions on Chapter 6

The most obvious theme to focus on when studying the impact of the First World War on the extension of the franchise is the extent of women's war work and its relationship to changing government attitudes. You also need to consider the work of the pre-war suffrage movement that did much to prepare the ground for votes for women. A number of examples of essay questions are given below:

1 Do you agree with the view that the First World War, 'far from facilitating votes for women actually postponed its implementation'? (*15 marks*)
2 Do you agree with the view expressed by Asquith on page 115 that women's suffrage was obtained because of their war efforts? (*15 marks*)
3 Do you agree with the view that 'the highly skilled and dangerous work done by women during the First World War was probably the greatest factor in the granting of the vote to women in February 1918'? (*15 marks*)
4 How valid is the view that the appointment to key government posts of several MPs sympathetic to women's suffrage led to the granting of votes to women? (*15 marks*)

These questions in the main require you to evaluate the proposition in the question against other contributory factors. When you are writing an essay a good introduction is essential. Your opening paragraph should form a bridge between the question and the answer and as such should contain a reference to the question. The core of your argument should form the bulk of the answer. Use paragraphs to develop your argument. While you will need to provide factual content, try to avoid providing a narrative account. For example, the proposition in question 4 makes the suggestion that the granting of the vote to women was the result of the work of sympathetic MPs as opposed to the work undertaken by the NUWSS and WSPU before the outbreak of war. How valid is this statement?

Always end your essay with a conclusion that draws together in summary form your response and highlights your judgement about the varying factors.

Source-based questions on Chapter 6

1 The Pankhursts 1914–18
Read carefully the sections in this chapter dealing with the role of the Pankhurst's in the First World War:

a) Use the evidence in this chapter to explain the role and importance of Sylvia Pankhurst during the First World War. (*4 marks*)

b) How and why did the work of Emmeline and Christabel Pankhurst differ from that of Sylvia Pankhurst? (*6 marks*)

c) To what extent were the splits in the WSPU in the war years the result of ideological differences between Sylvia Pankhurst and Christabel and Emmeline Pankhurst? (*10 marks*)

2 Asquith

Read carefully Asquith's speech to the House of Commons in 1917 on page 115.

a) Explain briefly what is meant by 'let the women work out their own salvation'? (*4 marks*)

b) Why did Asquith change his views during the war? (*6 marks*)

c) To what extent was Asquith's support for women's suffrage based on political compromise? (*10 marks*)

7 Conclusion: Life after Suffrage

POINTS TO CONSIDER

So was it all worth it? Did the vote bring about the changes that the suffragists and suffragettes yearned for? Many certainly thought so. Historians, of course, are more circumspect than suffrage activists because, with hindsight, they are able to evaluate the causes and consequences of significant historical events more clearly. From this vantage point you too can make a judgement about the extent to which the franchise accomplished what those who energetically campaigned for it had desired.

KEY DATES

1918   Constance Markiewicz elected to Parliament but did not take up her seat

1919   Nancy Astor became the first women MP to sit in Parliament; Sex Disqualification Act

1922   Married Women's Maintenance Act allowed women 40 shillings for herself and 10 shillings for each child; Infanticide Act removed the charge of murder from women found guilty of infanticide; Criminal Law Amendment Act removed the 'reasonable cause to believe' clause

1921   Six point group established; Marie Stopes opened first birth control clinic

1923   Matrimonial Causes Act allowed wives equal grounds for divorce; Bastardy Act increased maintenance payments to single mothers; five women elected as MPs

1925   Guardianship of Infants Act gave equal rights to men and women; Widows, Orphans and Old Age Contributory Pensions Act provided a pension and child allowances for widows of insured men.

1926   Equal Rights Demonstration

1928   Representation of the People Act gave vote to women on same terms as men

1969   Representation of the People Act gave vote to men and women over 18

1979   Margaret Thatcher becomes first woman Prime Minister

1 The Effects of the Vote

KEY ISSUE   Did the vote help women?

At first suffragists, elated at the prospect of voting, insisted that the vote had a tremendous significance for women's rights. To their minds, the enfranchisement of women would revolutionise government thinking as the voting power of the new electorate could not be ignored:

1 The Representation of the People Act had not been on the Statute Book a fortnight before the House of Commons discovered that every Bill which came before it had a 'woman's side', and the Party Whips began eagerly to ask 'what the women thought'. The ... House of
5 Commons, which had been firmly closed to all women since the early days of the militant agitation, was now opened, and access to Members became wonderfully easy. Letters from women constituents no longer went straight into waste-paparbaskets but received elaborate answers, and ... women's societies were positively welcomed at Westminster.[1]

Historians Martin Pugh and Olive Banks share this optimism and claim that, because of their newly acquired voting power, women achieved considerable gains. According to Pugh, there were 21 pieces of legislation between 1918 and 1929 that concerned women. Given these achievements, it is tempting to adopt a Whiggish approach to votes for women and represent women's advancements as an inevitable evolutionary process. History, however, is a little more like a roller-coaster than a straight railway track: women did not always achieve what they believed the franchise promised.

2 Effects on Parliament

> **KEY ISSUE** What effect did female suffrage have on Parliament?

In 1918 the Representation of the People Act was passed and for the first time in legal and political history a significant number of women had the opportunity to participate in the democratic process. Britain could now claim that she had a representative government as electoral democracy was no longer the preserve of men. After many years of struggle, Britain allegedly had a just and balanced government as the majority of the population was now enfranchised. But these views must be approached with some caution as women aged between 21 and 29 and even some women over the age of 30 were still denied the vote. Not until 1928 did women receive the vote on the same terms as men, thus properly marking the beginning of modern democracy in Britain (see pages 131–2).

Women may well have voted but they were slow in taking their places in the House of Commons. In the first election, in December 1918, 17 women, including a number of suffragists and suffragettes, stood for Parliament. All but one of the female candidates were

Women MPs on the terrace of the House of Commons. From the left are
Dorothy Jewson, Susan Lawrence, Nancy Astor, Margaret Wintringham,
Katherine Atholl, Mabel Philipson, Vera Terrington and
Margaret Bondfield.

defeated at the polls, including Christabel Pankhurst who stood as
Women's Party candidate at Smethwick, near Birmingham (the only
woman to receive official approval from the Coalition government),
Emmeline Pethick-Lawrence (Manchester) and Charlotte Despard
(Battersea North) both of whom stood as Labour candidates. The
only woman to be elected was Constance Markievicz who, because she
stood as a member of Sinn Fein (whose policy at the time was not to
recognise the British Government or its mechanisms), refused to take
her seat. Female parliamentary candidates, despite the enthusiastic
help they received from ex-suffrage activists, were in a weak position.
Women had no separate party machinery of their own with which to
contest seats. In addition they had limited financial resources with
which to fight their seats, were inexperienced in fighting elections
and were generally allocated unwinnable seats by the political parties
because the parties did not wish to give women one of their safer
seats. For example, Emmeline Pethick-Lawrence was supported by the
very small Labour Party in a predominantly Liberal stronghold. More
importantly, even though women had obtained the vote, the
country's electorate were not ready to vote for women MPs. Ironically,
the first woman MP to take her seat in the House of Commons (Nancy
Astor) got there when her husband, who had been Conservative MP
for Plymouth, was elevated to the peerage. Until then Nancy Astor

had not been interested in running for office but because Plymouth was regarded as the family seat of the Astors she was willing to take over from her husband.

Nancy Astor was the exception rather than the rule. In 1922 only 33 women were nominated as Parliamentary candidates out of a possible 615. By 1929 this had risen to 69, but it was hardly a significant figure especially when four out of five women stood in constituencies known to be hopeless for their particular parties and therefore had little chance of winning. Moreover, ten out of the 36 women who actually became MPs in this period gained their seats at by-elections rather than general elections, which suggests that their success may have as much to do with arbitrary factors such as voter dissatisfaction as with support for specifically female candidates. Furthermore, several Conservative women MPs owed their success, like Nancy Astor, to family connections rather than to feminist pressure.

Most women had the legal right to become MPs but social convention generally denied them the opportunity. Until August 1917 women had to listen to debates behind a grille in the Ladies' Gallery so that the male MPs would not be distracted by the female form and the women would be protected from male glances. The grille was removed but women's role in 1920 was still perceived to be in their own house looking after their family not in the House of Commons looking after the country. As a consequence, the predominantly all-male selection committees feared that women might alienate the electorate and were unwilling to accept them as prospective MPs. Indeed, Conservative selection Committees looked for husband and wife teams where the men would be MPs and the women (naturally!) would act in a supportive capacity, organising fêtes and bazaars to raise money and entertaining the party faithful. Not surprisingly, when Nancy Astor made her first entrance in the House of Commons she made quite a stir. Winston Churchill, who had often visited her Cliveden home, ignored her and when challenged said he found her presence in the House of Commons as embarrassing as if she had entered his bathroom when he was naked. Nancy replied 'Nonsense, Winston, you are not good-looking enough to have fears of this sort'. Nancy Astor spoke often, and well, but never forgot the basic principles of traditional femininity: she was always soberly dressed and never visited the male preserves of the Smoking Room in case she offended the other MPs.

Once in Parliament, women began to be appointed to official Government posts. In 1924 Margaret Bondfield was appointed Parliamentary Secretary at the Ministry of Labour in the short-lived Labour Government. Not to be outdone, the Conservatives appointed Katherine Atholl as Parliamentary Secretary of State at the Board of Education when they replaced the Labour Government in the same year. Meanwhile the new female MPs were busy establishing links that cut across party lines and trying to promote legislation to advance women's rights. The photograph on page 124 shows eight female MPs who were in the House of Commons in 1924. Dorothy Jewson (Labour), former member of the WSPU, a pacifist and trade union organiser, spent time on promoting health and housing issues and helped form the Workers' Birth Control Group, which tried to persuade the Labour Party to adopt a policy of free birth control advice. Susan Lawrence (Labour), a former trade union organiser, helped guide the Widows, Orphans and Old Age Pensioners' Bill through Parliament. Nancy Astor (Conservative) became known for her commitment to the principles of equal franchise, pensions, better education and working conditions, marriage property reform, legislation to protect young children and temperance reform. Margaret Wintringham (Liberal), former NUWSS member, campaigned for an extension of women's suffrage, the right of women to sit in the House of Lords, provision of state scholarships for girls, equal pay and women-only railway carriages. Katherine Atholl (Conservative) spoke against genital mutilation in Africa and Mabel Philipson (Conservative) was active on the Select Committee that framed legislation to give married women rights over their own children. Vera Terrington (Liberal) was in Parliament for less than a year so had little effect. Margaret Bondfield (Labour) was a former trade union activist who campaigned for women's rights, supported adult suffrage and later became the first woman Cabinet Minister. Absent from the photograph is Ellen Wilkinson (Labour) who was elected for Middlesborough East in 1924. Ellen Wilkinson, soon dubbed 'Red Ellen' both for her left-wing politics and the colour of her hair, had been an NUWSS district organiser, a pacifist during the war and a trade union official who was active in the 1926 General Strike. Virulently anti-Conservative and committed to left-wing policies, Ellen Wilkinson became a devoted friend of Nancy Astor's, thus once again illustrating the commitment of these new MPs to work across party lines in support of women's issues.

However, neither the enfranchisement of women nor the election of female MPs changed the nature of Parliamentary politics. Suffragists and suffragettes had hoped that, once women achieved the vote, they would make a distinctive contribution to the political arena by 'feminising' politics. It was believed that women would bring special skills to Parliament that would make the confrontational style of party politics disappear in favour of politics based on principles. This wish was not fulfilled. The House of Commons remained 'essentially a man's institution evolved through centuries by men to deal with men's affairs in a man's way'.[2] Men dominated in the House of Commons in their style of politics as they did in sheer weight of numbers. The election of women MPs neither brought about a new age nor 'feminised' the political process, as women merely adapted to the masculine style of the House of Commons, learning debating skills and an adversarial approach. Overall, women MPs failed to make a distinctive stand over women's issues and some of the women MPs with feminist sympathies, like Margaret Bondfield, were forced to compromise their feminism or else become marginalised within party politics.

b) Effects on Women's Work

KEY ISSUE How did the vote affect women's work?

Suffragists and suffragettes had wanted the vote partly to widen women's employment opportunities, increase their pay and improve their working conditions. To some extent they had their wishes fulfilled, at least in the legal sense. In 1919, as a direct result of women's franchise, the Sex Disqualification Removal Act stated that 'a person should not be disqualified by sex or marriage from the exercise of any public function or from being appointed or holding any civil or judicial office or post or from entering or assuming or carrying on any civil profession or vocation'. This allowed women to take up civil service and judicial posts, become barristers or magistrates and serve on juries. The Act opened the legal profession to women like Christabel Pankhurst who had studied law but had not been allowed to practise it except in her own defence. It also allowed women to become chartered accountants and bankers. Certainly in the 1920s there were a number of significant firsts: the first woman to qualify as a veterinary surgeon; the first woman pilot to enter an air race; the first female British delegate to the League of Nations; the first woman solicitor; the first woman barrister; the first jurywomen; the first female JP; the first woman deacon in the Church of England; and the first woman Cabinet Minister.

Women may have been granted the legal right to enter previously male professions but they made insignificant inroads. Despite the vote, most work was as much characterised by a sexual division of labour in 1928 as it had been over 60 years before. Many professions continued to be male-dominated. In 1919 many of the London teaching hospitals still refused to train women doctors; in 1920 when the Civil Service was re-organised, women remained excluded from high office; and by 1927 only a small number of women had been appointed as JPs. Greater opportunities emerged for middle-class women in the teaching and clerical professions but women were rarely given the top jobs. As one President of the National Association of Schoolmasters declared in 1934, 'Only a nation heading for a madhouse would force upon men ... such a position as service under a spinster headmistress.'[3] And when the expansion of the white-blouse worker – the department store shop assistant, the nurse and the clerk – offered women employment opportunities this owed more to technological and educational advances than to the vote.

Moreover, employers often ignored the 1919 Sexual Disqualification Removal Act and obliged women to resign when they married. In the 1920s about three-quarters of all local authorities operated a marriage bar for women teachers and many public health authorities dismissed married female doctors and nurses; similarly women civil servants were given a dowry and forced to leave once they married. The decision not to employ married women was justified because 'women could not service two masters',[4] that is their husbands and their bosses, at the same time.

Votes for women did little for working-class women as there continued to be a high degree of sexual segregation in working-class occupations. Domestic service or agricultural labour remained the only two options available to working-class rural women until well after the Second World War. Once again, even when women worked in the same areas as men, they were found in the lower grades of those occupations, being over-represented in unskilled rather than skilled jobs. New opportunities did occur for women in the new light industries but these, like those of the white blouse workers, were the effect of technological change rather than the effect of the vote.

More importantly, women remained a cheap and easily exploitable workforce as their work commanded lower rates of pay than men, whether they were middle class or working class. Despite a campaign to obtain equal pay, female teachers' salaries were set one-fifth lower than men's by the Standing Joint Committee on Teachers' Salaries. Similarly women civil servants were paid 75 per cent of male salaries as a rule. In all-female middle-class occupations women were worse off. Nursing, for example, was seen as a vocation rather than a career, so women were paid low salaries in order to attract middle-class women who did not need to work for a living. Working-class women fared little better, for they continued to receive wages roughly half those of men.

One is therefore led to believe that although women had gained political power through the ballot box, economic power was still held by men. The justification for this inequality can be traced to the ideology of domesticity whereby women were perceived as wives and mothers rather than workers. Indeed, Martin Pugh claims that it was commonly held that working women deprived men of jobs – one manufacturer even advocated the dismissal of women workers in order to solve the unemployment problem. Women's pay was not surprisingly viewed as 'pin-money', a supplement to the wages of husbands, rather than a living wage. As a consequence, women were denied the economic equality that feminists continued to demand. However, in fairness, it should be recognised that there was a consistently high level of overall unemployment in the inter-war period: unemployment never fell below 1 million and reached 3 million at its height.

c) Effects on Marriage and the Family

> **KEY ISSUE** To what extent did the vote help promote marital equality?

Post-war politicians promised to create homes fit for heroes and feminists wanted no less themselves. High hopes were held that women's suffrage might not only act as a legal protection against husbands but might help promote equality in marriage. There were some notable successes in this area. Largely as a result of feminist pressure, the Matrimonial Causes Act of 1923 allowed a wife to divorce her husband on grounds of adultery, thus ending a long history of double standards for men and women. However, wives did not benefit entirely from this new legislation – one historian suggests that it made sex more of a duty for wives than it had before. Two years later, in 1925, the Guardianship of Infants Act completed the work of nineteenth-century feminists by placing mothers and fathers in an equal position with regard to custody of their children. In the same year, husbands were no longer held responsible for any criminal act committed by their wives in their presence. In effect, this act consolidated women's position as independent beings who were outside the control and jurisdiction of their husbands. Once divorced, women who wished to stay in the marital home found they had no claim to it even though they were not the 'guilty' party. Furthermore, courts (with male judges) generally examined the conduct of women, just as much as their financial needs, before assessing their claim to maintenance.

In order to redress these economic and domestic inequalities, many feminists became concerned with 'welfare feminism' in the 1920s.[5] In 1919 the NUWSS changed its name to the National Union of Societies for Equal Citizenship (NUSEC) and, under the leadership of the independent MP Eleanor Rathbone, campaigned for social reforms. Rather than struggle for equal pay with men, it was suggested that married women be given a family allowance if they cared for their children at home. In this way, women's unpaid work in the home would at last be financially recognised and rewarded. The leadership of NUSEC believed that family allowances would not only give married women some measure of financial independence but would strengthen the position of single women. With money paid directly to women with children, there would be little justification for men being paid a 'family wage' and thus more than women. Equal pay for equal work would therefore be brought about.

Not surprisingly, many feminists disagreed with this approach to women's rights. This 'new' feminism, with its emphasis on welfare at the expense of equality, was seen, for a number of reasons, as a betrayal rather than a continuation of feminism. Firstly, feminists such as Millicent Fawcett disagreed with family allowances because they consolidated, rather than challenged, women's home-making and child-rearing roles. Secondly, family allowances diverted women from the struggle for equal pay in the public world by offering them a bribe to stay at home. Thirdly, family allowances might depress working-class wages in general because the state subsidised families with children and there was therefore little incentive for employers to raise salaries in line with the cost of living. Finally, feminists dismissed family allowances as nonsense because they advocated an ideal family of three children, whereas few families were like this.

d) Effects on Sexual Morality

> **KEY ISSUE** What impact did the vote have on sexual morality?

Suffragists and suffragettes also wanted the vote to protect young girls from sexual assault, to eliminate venereal disease, to curb unfair legislation against prostitutes, and to ensure a single moral standard for both sexes. Once again, they enjoyed only a limited success as the following evidence will show. Feminists achieved a small victory when the 1922 Criminal Law Amendment Act abolished the 'reasonable cause to believe' clause. Under the old Act, men who had seduced a girl under 16 were able to claim that they had not realised that she was under age and thus avoided conviction. However, the new Act was limited in scope as it only applied to full sexual intercourse and not to indecent assault.

The extent of venereal disease continued to cause alarm. Emmeline Pankhurst spent a lot of time in North America lecturing on the dangers of venereal disease, but the women's movement in Britain seemed to reserve judgement on the subject. However, the British Social Hygiene Council made strenuous efforts to curb its spread and several films were produced – *The Girl Who Doesn't Know, Damaged Goods, The Flaw* – to educate people on the disease itself. In the 1920s Manchester City Council opened venereal clinics in public lavatories but these were quickly closed as a result of feminist and other public disapproval. And of course it was the discovery of penicillin, rather than women's moral crusading, which diminished the rate of venereal infection.

Feminist social purists certainly had friends in high places to help them establish sexual moral standards: one film censor later became President of the National Vigilance Association (a group of men and women committed to social purity) and one Home Secretary in the 1920s undertook to improve public sexual morality. As a consequence, there was rigid sexual censorship: books such as Radclyffe Hall's *Well of Loneliness* about lesbianism either faced prosecution or were not distributed and thus quietly disappeared. A woman's police force was also established to advise young girls on moral matters and investigate sex offences.

In 1925 Nancy Astor introduced a bill to reform the law on soliciting and prostitution. At the time, women could be convicted of soliciting purely on the word of a police officer, and then fined or sent to prison. Soliciting – not prostitution – was an offence so men were never charged with kerb-crawling. Incensed at this injustice, Astor advocated equality between the sexes in relation to prostitution offences and the elimination of the term 'common' prostitute from the legal code. Her efforts led to a Department Committee of Inquiry on Street Offences 1927 but the Parliamentary bills she put forward never reached the statute book.

It could be argued that the double sexual standard, so criticised by both suffragists and suffragettes, was replaced by an even lower single standard in that there was a decline in female sexual morality rather than an improvement in male morality. Indeed, some feminists supported the Association for Moral and Social Hygiene, an organisation descended from Josephine Butler's Ladies' National Association, which campaigned to raise the age of consent to 18 years. Others criticised this and the moral puritanism of the pre-war suffragettes and instead advocated women's right to sexual pleasure. As a consequence, the campaigns they led were different ones. It was believed that women could not enjoy sex because of a fear of pregnancy, so the birth control movement won favour amongst many new wave feminists. Birth control, promoted by Marie Stopes who set up the first birth control clinic in 1921 in Holloway, London, enabled women to take control of their own sexuality, or – as some like Nancy Astor feared – be as irresponsible as men.

e) Effects on the Women's Movement

> **KEY ISSUE** What happened to the women's movement after a limited vote was achieved?

Some historians claim that the women's movement declined after 1918 as few campaigners remained fully committed to extending votes for women on the same terms as men. However, this is not the case. Although the suffrage movement was not as strong as it had been pre-war, many women remained actively involved. Certainly, the suffragists kept up a quiet pressure on the Government throughout this time, continuously pointing out the illogicality of the 1918 decision. Yet their story is only just being written: most historians end their work in 1918 and ignore the 10 years after women gained a limited franchise. However, it is safe to say that further franchise reform was not a priority of either most feminists or the government. In many ways it was a 'tidying up' process that happened almost accidentally when a Conservative Minister gave a commitment to equal franchise during a rather lively public meeting. The Prime Minister,

Stanley Baldwin, felt he should honour this promise, and fearful that if the Conservatives didn't reform the vote, Labour would, another 5 million young women or so were added to the voting register.

It is often argued that once women had achieved a limited franchise in 1918, feminism lost its vital spark. Without any political direction it degenerated into a small number of fragmented organisations. But, as Sheila Jeffreys points out, this fails to give weight to the other concerns of feminists. Once the vote had been achieved, there were a myriad of organisations that either lobbied for single issue campaigns – such as the Equal Pay Campaign Committee, the Association for Moral and Social Hygiene, and the Housewives' League – or acted as an umbrella organisation, such as the National Council for Women, the National Union of Societies for Equal Citizenship and the Six Point Group. In many ways, post-war feminism, with its diverse campaigning, was the true heir of Victorian feminism.

Certainly, some of the leaders of the WSPU sank into political oblivion once the vote had been achieved. Christabel Pankhurst made a concerted effort to remain in the political fray by standing for the first Parliament; she then enjoyed a brief spell as a journalist before turning to Second Adventism and Christian religious revivalism. Her mother remained active, leading a campaign against venereal disease in Canada before returning to stand as Conservative Parliamentary candidate for Whitechapel but she never attracted huge audiences again. Annie Kenney married in 1921 and retired from public life. 'Slasher Mary' (see page 71) joined the British Union of Fascists. Meanwhile, the leadership of the other organisations not only continued to press for universal suffrage but remained politically active in left-wing causes. Sylvia Pankhurst helped to found the British Communist Party, championed an anti-Fascist crusade and emigrated to Ethiopia where she became a friend and political advisor to Haile Selassie. Charlotte Despard stood as Parliamentary Candidate for Battersea in the first election but her major energy was directed to working for Irish independence. She remained committed to radical socialist policies throughout the rest of her life and, at the age of 91, addressed an anti-Nazi rally in Hyde Park. The Pethick-Lawrences both became Labour party activists, with Fred even defeating Winston Churchill in the 1923 election. Millicent Fawcett, though no longer leader of the NUWSS, campaigned for greater work opportunities and legal justice for women. Subsequent decades, Martin Pugh argues, actually saw the waning of the impact of women's enfranchisement as the leading figures of the suffrage movement grew old and faded from the political scene. Indeed, when women finally achieved equal suffrage with men this was not followed by any immediate advances in women's position – but maybe this was due to the fact that Britain was about to enter a depression.

Contemporary Britain is still characterised – to some extent – by male dominance within parliamentary politics, the economic inequalities that women suffer and the popular expectation that women's place is in the home. In such a context it is all too easy to be cynical about the enfranchisement of women. Power, it is argued, no longer rests in Parliament but in commerce and finance. The failure of the franchise to realise the hopes of the suffragists and the suffragettes, it is said, illustrates the limitations of the vote to effect change. Nevertheless, the franchise should not be dismissed as 'marking a cross on a piece of paper' for it not only acts as a check on government and makes those in government answerable to the electorate, but has the authority to change the economic framework of society. Governments may have failed to satisfy the demands of British feminists between the wars but the position of women in Italy and Germany, where democracy collapsed, was calamitous. Furthermore, one only has to think of the nationalisation of the 1940s, the subsequent denationalisation of the 1980s and 1990s and the Labour landslide victory of 1997 to appreciate the immense power that Parliament still enjoys. And women, who represent over 50 per cent of the electorate, certainly have the capability to change the composition of Parliament and with it the political direction of Britain.

References

1 *The Cause,* Ray Strachey (Virago Press, 1978), p. 367.
2 *Separate Spheres: The Opposition to Women's Suffrage in Britain,* Brian Harrison (Croom Helm, 1978) p. 234.
3 *Women in England, 1870–1950,* Jane Lewis (Wheatsheaf, 1984), p. 190.
4 *Feminism and the Family in England, 1880–1929,* Carol Dyhouse (Basil Blackwell, 1989), p. 79.
5 *Faces of Feminism,* Olive Banks (Blackwell, 1986).

Summary Diagram
The impact of the vote on women

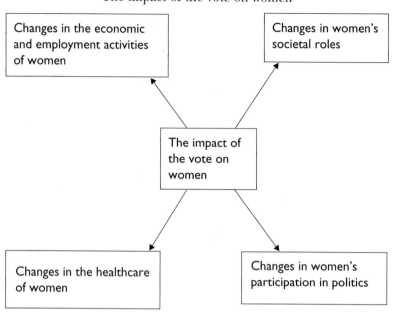

Changes in the economic and employment activities of women

Changes in women's societal roles

The impact of the vote on women

Changes in the healthcare of women

Changes in women's participation in politics

Working on Chapter 7

It is assumed that by the time you read this chapter you will be nearing the end of your unit of study. You will have studied *Votes for Women* in some depth and should have a good understanding of what actually occurred in the nineteenth century and the early part of the twentieth. Your studies should not only have covered issues relevant to the struggle for the vote but also the wider issues surrounding the role of women in the nineteenth and early part of the twentieth century and how this worked against them gaining political recognition. This chapter draws together the implications of this struggle on the daily lives of all women, including employment rights, birth control and many other factors that affect women. Finally this chapter will allow you to address the issue of change over time and in particular what the consequences of the different events were. One approach that you might consider, to help your understanding of the nature and scale of the changes caused by the granting of the vote to women, is to construct a grid. In one column consider the position of women before the 1918 Representation of People Act, while in another column note what changes occurred during the twentieth century.

Answering essay and structured questions on Chapter 7

The content of this chapter is likely to provide examiners with an opportunity to devise synoptic type questions. In the present examination structure, these questions will be set at the end of your course on the A Level paper. Synoptic assessment principally seeks to assess the full range of skills and ideas developed through the study of other AS and A level units. This unit will be source based, with a mixture of sources. The question will be phrased as a proposition for you to argue against or for, using the sources provided and your own knowledge.

1   Using the evidence in the section 'Effects on Parliament' answer the following questions:
  a) 'For the first time in legal and political history, women had the opportunity to participate equally in the democratic process.' Using the evidence and your own knowledge, how far do you agree with this view? (*10 marks*)
  b) 'Neither the enfranchisement of women nor the election of female MPs changed the nature of Parliamentary politics.' Using your own knowledge and the evidence in the source, explain how far you agree with this interpretation of the impact of women's votes on Parliament. (*20 marks*)

2   Using the evidence in 'Effects on Women's Work' answer the following questions:
  a) 'Women may have been granted the legal right to enter previously male professions but they made insignificant inroads.' Using the evidence and your own knowledge explain why. (*10 marks*)
  b) 'One is led to believe that although women had gained political power through the ballot box, economic power was still held by men.' Using the evidence of the source and your own knowledge explain how far you agree with this statement. (*20 marks*)

To answer these questions you will need to focus carefully on the sources and make a note of the reasons put forward. You will then need to consider other factors that may have a bearing on your argument whether it agrees or disagrees with the view. Then you need to make a judgement on which of the factors is the most important. For example, in question **2b)**, you will need to discuss why economic power was still held by men, particularly in the inter-war years.

Essay questions will examine themes and you will be expected to show the connections between different periods or events. The following are examples of possible questions:

1   'The First World War was the key factor influencing the changing role of women and subsequently led to their gaining the right to vote.' How far do you agree with this view? (*15 marks*)

2   Explain how before 1914 the Liberals appealed to, but also antagonised, the women's suffrage movement. (*15 marks*)

Further Reading

A large number of books have been written on women's suffrage, so the list below merely offers a guide to the most accessible and important texts. Where a book has only been mentioned by the author in the text, the full source details will be found below.

1 Primary Sources

Many of the autobiographical memoirs and histories written by suffragists have been reprinted, allowing student access to valuable primary source material. Christabel Pankhurst's *Unshackled* (Hutchinson, 1959), Emmeline Pankhurst's *My Own Story* (Virago, 1979), Sylvia Pankhurst's *The Suffragette Movement* (Virago, 1977) and Ray Strachey's *The Cause* (Virago, 1978) are useful for student research projects because they were written by those actively engaged in the campaign for votes for women and provide insights into the minds of the important leaders of women's suffrage. For example in *My Own Story* the reader is made aware of Emmeline Pankhurst's enormous physical energy and emotional drive, as well as her developing political awareness. Nevertheless, autobiographies and histories written by those involved in the women's suffrage movement must be used with care. Emmeline Pankhurst's book was in fact written by an American journalist and contains many factual errors. Although Ray Strachey's book seems much more reasoned than that of Emmeline Pankhurst it must be remembered that she was a leading figure of the NUWSS and thus writes more favourably about them than about the WSPU.

There are also useful primary source collections. Two of the most important are from the Women's Source Library. The first book, *Before the Vote was Won: Arguments For and Against Women's Suffrage 1864–1896* (Routledge and Kegan Paul, 1987), edited by Jane Lewis, traces the arguments mainly of those in support of women's suffrage, whereas the second, *Suffrage and the Pankhurst* (Routledge and Kegan Paul, 1987), edited by Jane Marcus, includes many useful articles, documents and pamphlets written by and about the Women's Social and Political Union. Both have interesting and thought-provoking introductions to the source material.

2 Secondary Sources

The suffragettes used to dominate the histories of the struggle for votes for women. Most of these were written by men. George

Dangerfield's highly provocative *The Strange Death of Liberal England* (Perigree, 1980), which was first published in 1935, offers a scurrilously unsympathetic yet magnificently written account of the suffragette movement. For entertainment value alone Dangerfield is worth a read, but those sympathetic to feminism might be offended by his interpretation. Unfortunately, much of Dangerfield's style has been reproduced by other historians who found it difficult to remain uninfluenced by his interpretative stance and style of writing. For example, David Mitchell's equally readable *The Fighting Pankhursts* (Jonathan Cape, 1967) examines the WSPU leadership in some detail but trivialises the political motivation of the suffragette leaders. Similarly, Roger Fulford's *Votes for Women* (Faber and Faber, 1957), which recounts the wider story of the suffragists as well as the suffragettes, belittles their achievements. In contrast, Andrew Rosen's *Rise Up Women* (Routledge and Kegan Paul, 1974) provides a scholarly narrative of the suffragette movement based on extensive research. This is a good analytical narrative of the suffragette movement which is well worth reading.

Some of the earliest and most important books to place women's suffrage within a wider political context are Constance Rover's *Women's Suffrage and Party Politics in Britain, 1866–1914* (Routledge and Kegan Paul, 1967), David Morgan's more specialist *Suffragists and Liberals* (Basil Blackwell, 1975), Martin Pugh's *Electoral Reform in War and Peace, 1906–1918* (Routledge and Kegan Paul, 1978) and Brian Harrison's *Separate Spheres* (Croom Helm, 1978). The first three of these books examine the relationship of the women's suffrage movement to the main political parties and to political reform, while the third analyses the opposition to women's suffrage. All four are excellent scholarly works which, although written some time ago, do not demean women's struggle for the vote.

The birth and growth of feminist politics brought new interpretations of suffrage history. One of the first two historians to break both new empirical and methodological ground is Jill Liddington's and Jill Norris's *One Hand Tied Behind Us* (Virago, 1978). Liddington and Norris use local archives to construct an account of working-class suffragists active in the cotton towns of northern England. This book has done more than any other to break away from the belief that the suffrage movement was full of middle-class women. Yet, although Liddington and Norris have reinstated the suffragists in the story of votes for women, they are much too dismissive of the WSPU and tend to see the Pankhursts in a similar way to Dangerfield.

A recent renewal of interest in the suffrage movement has produced a range of new material. Elizabeth Crawford's *The Women's Suffrage Movement* (Routledge, 1999) is an excellent and much needed reference guide to the wide variety of groups and individuals who made up the movement. A number of authors have re-evaluated the campaign for votes for women. Mary Joannou and June Purvis, *The Women's*

Suffrage Movement: New Feminist Perspectives (Manchester University Press, 1998), June Purvis and Sandra Stanley Holton, *Votes for Women* (Routledge, 2000), Claire Eustance, Joan Ryan and Laura Ugolini, *A Suffrage Reader* (Leicester University Press, 2000) all provide introductions to the major current debates within suffrage history. Lesley P. Hume's *The National Union of Women's Suffrage Societies* (Garland, 1982) and Sandra Stanley Holton's *Feminism and Democracy* (Cambridge University Press, 1986) both provide a useful antidote to the Pankhurstian tradition by concentrating on the constitutionalist wing of the suffrage movement. Holton, in particular, offers a new perspective on suffrage history by placing the campaign for the vote within the wider framework of social reform politics. Martin Pugh's very readable *The March of Women* (Oxford University Press, 2000) shares a similar approach to both Hulme and Holton and draws extensively on their findings. Hilda Kean's *Deeds Not Words: the Lives of Suffragette Teachers* (Pluto Press, 1990) is an evocative account which also challenges the Pankhurst myth.

There is a trend within feminist historiography to place the suffrage movement within the context of sexual politics. Susan Kingsley Kent's *Sex and Suffrage in Britain, 1860–1914* (Routledge, 1987) is a key book here. Suffrage history, however, has concentrated on women: where men are mentioned it is in opposition to women's suffrage. The only book, so far, to examine men's support of women's suffrage is A.V. John's and Claire Eustance's edited *The Men's Share* (Routledge, 1997). This important book examines who these men were, the organisations they established and how they organised their support.

For those who enjoy reading biographies, Jill Liddington's *The Life and Times of a Respectable Rebel, Selina Cooper, 1864–1946* (Virago, 1984), B. Harrison's *Prudent Revolutionaries* (Clarendon Press, 1987), Angela John's *Elizabeth Robins: Staging a Life* (Routledge, 1995), Sandra Stanley Holton's *Suffrage Day: Stories from the Women's Suffrage Movement* (Routledge, 1996), Verna Coleman's *Adela Pankhurst* (Melbourne University Press, 1996), Barbara Winslow's, *Sylvia Pankhurst* (UCL, 1996), Martin Pugh's, *The Pankhursts* (Penguin, 2001), Paula Bartley's *Emmeline Pankhurst* (Routledge, 2002) and June Purvis's *Emmeline Pankhurst, a biography* (Routledge, 2002) are perhaps the most valuable.

Despite this increase in output on women's suffrage, most books on the suffrage movement have concentrated on England. To redress this imbalance Leah Leneman's *A Guid Cause* (Aberdeen University Press, 1991) and Cliona Murphy's *The Women's Suffrage Movement and Irish Society in the Early Twentieth Century* (Harvester Wheatsheaf, 1989) examine the suffrage movement in Scotland and Ireland. They argue that whereas the suffrage movement in Scotland mirrored the English experience, the Irish struggle for votes for women was uniquely different. In a seminal article by Catherine Hall, 'Rethinking Imperial Histories: The Reform Act of 1867' in *New Left Review* (1994), it is even argued that the British women's suffrage movement cannot be understood outside a global context of imperialism. Indeed, the British women's suffrage movement was part of a wider international suffrage movement which M. Nolan's and C. Daley's edited collection *Suffrage and Beyond, International Perspectives* (Auckland University Press, 1994) examines. An excellent recent study by June Hannam, Katherine Holden and Mitzi Auchterlonie, *International Encyclopaedia of Women's Suffrage* (ABC Clio, 2000) further reminds us that votes for women was an international campaign.

Of course, life did not end with the vote. Four useful books which evaluate women's achievements post-1918 are Joanna Alberti's *Beyond Suffrage* (Macmillan, 1989), Martin Pugh's *Women and the Women's Movement in Britain, 1914–1959* (Macmillan, 1992), Cheryl Power's *Suffrage and Power* (I.B. Tauris, 1997) and – in the *Access to History* series – Annette Mayer's *Women in Britain 1900–2000* (Hodder & Stoughton, 2002).

Index

Actresses Franchise League 49, 61, 62

Anti-suffragists 10, 21–6, 50, 67, 82, 97–9, 115

Atkinson, Di 61, 99

Asquith 64, 65, 70, 82–3, 101, 115, 118

Becker, Lydia 17, 33–4, 35, 37, 50, 57, 60, 63, 66

'Black Friday' 71, 87–8

Bodichon, Barbara 3, 33, 34, 37, 50

Campbell-Bannerman 64, 82

'Cat and Mouse Act' 90–2, 97

Central Committee of the National Society for Women's Suffrage (CCWS) 34, 35, 39

Churchill, Winston 25, 64–5, 83, 87, 91, 97, 125

Conciliation Bills 55, 70, 74, 79, 80, 83

Conservative Party 7, 37, 45, 80–2, 116, 125–6

Contagious Diseases Acts 1, 6, 16, 18, 34, 37, 93

Davison, Emily 33, 70

Despard, Charlotte 45, 46, 69, 109, 124, 132

Disraeili, Benjamin 25, 81

East London Federation of Suffragettes (ELFS) 42, 46, 92, 95–6, 108–9, 118

Elmy, Elizabeth Wolstenholme 5, 33, 36, 37

Fawcett, Millicent 17, 20, 35, 37, 39, 43, 59, 109–10, 129, 132

Forcible feeding 89–90, 92

Gladstone, William 24, 25, 82

Hardie, Keir 65, 84

Harrison, Brian 21, 67, 97

Holton, Sandra 55, 97, 118

Hunger striking 47, 73–4, 89

Irish Women's Franchise League (IWFL) 49

Kenney, Annie 40, 43, 64–5, 132

Labour Party 37, 43, 45, 65, 80, 83–5, 91, 116, 125, 126

Lancashire and Cheshire Women Textile and Other Workers Representation Committee (LCWT) 38

Liberal Party 7, 64, 65, 66, 68, 74–5, 82–3, 85–91, 116, 126

Liddington, Jill and Norris, Jill 16, 37, 40, 43, 91

Lloyd George, David 64–5, 71, 83, 99, 107, 115, 118

Lytton, Constance 43, 50, 71, 73

MacDonald, Ramsay 84

Men's Federation for Women's Suffrage 94–5

Men's League for Women's Suffrage 84, 94–5

Militancy 56, 64–73

Munition workers 113

National Society for Women's Suffrage (NSWS) 32, 34

National Union of Women's Suffrage Societies (NUWSS) 18, 20, 36–9, 41–3, 46–7, 49, 56–9, 63–4, 69, 85, 94–6, 106, 109–12, 118, 126, 129

Pankhurst, Christabel 6, 17–18, 27, 36, 40–3, 45–6, 64, 93, 106–7, 124, 132

Pankhurst, Emmeline 7, 17, 35–6, 40–8, 70–1, 74–5, 95–6, 105–7, 130,

Pankhurst, Richard 11, 35–6, 63, 66, 82

Pankhurst, Sylvia 40, 42–3, 45–6, 84, 92, 108–9, 132

Pethick-Lawrence, Emmeline 40, 45–6, 50, 59, 97, 108–9, 124, 132

Pethick-Lawrence, Frederick 21, 42, 45, 46, 83, 124, 132

Parliamentary reform (men) 10, 13–14

Parliamentary reform (women) 1, 6, 123

Pugh, Martin 62, 181, 95, 117, 123, 128, 132

Purvis, June 88

Suffragettes 1, 11, 15, 27–8, 32, 40–8, 56, 61–73, 126–7

Suffragists 1, 11, 14–17, 27–8, 32–9, 48–9, 55–6, 62–3, 126–7, 131

Ward, Mrs Humphrey 23, 25, 28, 31, 50, 74–5, 89–90

Women's Freedom League (WFL) 32, 45–6, 69, 96, 109

Women's Social and Political Union (WSPU) 13, 17, 19, 20, 32, 36, 40–9, 55, 57–9, 61–2, 64, 84–5, 87, 93–5, 105–7, 126, 132